Object Analysis and Design

Comparison of Methods

Andrew T. F. Hutt, EDITOR

A Wiley–QED Publication

John Wiley & Sons, Inc.

New York • Chichester • Brisbane • Toronto • Singapore

Contents

Preface

PURPOSE

This report contains the results of the survey of object analysis and design methods which was conducted by the OMG Object Analysis and Design Special Interest Group between October 1992 and January 1993.

It has been developed as part of the Object Management Group's drive to establish a common understanding of object technology.

READERS

This document is intended for those who are interested in object analysis and design methods either as developers or as users of such methods.

STRUCTURE

This document is in three parts:

- *Part A: Introduction* describes the Object Analysis and Design Special Interest Group and criteria used in the survey.
- *Part B: Survey Results* contains the results of the survey.
- *Part C: Technical Framework* describes the model of object analysis and design that the group created in order to survey the available methods.

The appendix lists the responses produced by the methods suppliers.

STATUS

This document is a working document of the OMG Object Analysis and Design Special Interest Group. It is being published so that others can access the wealth of information that this survey has produced.

The document is not a comparative evaluation of methods and is not judgmental. It does not recommend a best method; it merely attempts to find out about the methods for object analysis and design. It is not intended to address several important aspects necessary for evaluation and selection for an organization like the process or modeling languages used in the method and its relationship to project management.

The document should not used as a textbook for introducing object analysis and design.

The document should be viewed as a source of information and broad review of existing methods, but should not be interpreted as exhaustive or as being based on fully defined concepts. The authors and editors of this material hope the work continues to be clarified and expanded in technical content.

ACKNOWLEDGMENTS

This document was produced by the OMG Object Analysis and Design Special Interest Group.

Chairman: Object Analysis and Design Special Interest Group

A. T. F. Hutt   International Computers Limited

Document editors

Claude Baudoin	Sematech
Magnus Christerson	Objective Systems
John Dodd	Texas Instruments
Gary Fine	Intellicorp
Geir Hoeydalsvik	University of Trondheim
Denise Lynch	United Technologies, Pratt and Whitney
Karen Oppel	Software AG
Yves Patoureaux	Telesystems
Kenny Rubin	ParcPlace Systems
Brad Kain	Semaphore
Peter Thomas	Oracle UK
Elaine Ward	MITRE CORPORATION
George Wilkie	University of Ulster

Other people who participated in the Special Interest Group are:

Eric Aranow	CASElode Consulting
R. Bahlye	Software A G
D. Beech	Oracle

D. Belisle	IBM
F. Campagnoni	IBM
M. Goldberg	Rational Europe
K. Murphy	James Martin & Co.
G. L. Hollowell	Texas Instruments
M. A. Lenzi	Syrinx Corporation
P. Thompson	Unisys
D. Vines	NEC America

People outside the Special Interest Group who provided material for this document are:

E. Aranow	CASElode Consulting
G. Berrisford	Object Models on behalf of CCTA
P. DiPietro	Olivetti Information Systems
I. Graham	BIS Information Systems
K. Lano, H. Haughton	Lloyds Register
K. J. Lieberherr	Northeastern University, Boston
D. Redmond-Pyle	LBMS
I. White	Rational
A. Wills	Object Engineering

Finally I would like to thank Miss S. Holst from Department of Psychology, Nottingham University, who spent time and effort preparing the survey questionnaire.

Andrew Hutt

Introduction

Overview of Survey

1.1 OBJECT MANAGEMENT GROUP

This document was published by the Object Management Group (OMG). It was produced by the Object Analysis and Design Special Interest Group, which is part of the OMG.

The OMG is dedicated to maximizing the portability, reusability, and interoperability of software. The OMG is the leading worldwide organization dedicated to producing a framework and specifications for commercially available object environments.

The Object Management Architecture Guide provides a statement of OMG's architecture for object-oriented systems.

The Object Analysis and Design Special Interest Group is concerned with the methods used in the analysis and design of object-oriented systems.

1.2 OBJECT ANALYSIS AND DESIGN SPECIAL INTEREST GROUP

The mission of this group is to advance the technology and awareness of object analysis and design, to encourage the development of applications which exploit the Object Management Architecture.

The short-term objectives of the group are:

- To develop a technical framework for object analysis and design
- To publish a description of existing object analysis and design methods
- To publish a survey of existing object analysis and design methods

1.3   THE TECHNICAL FRAMEWORK

This technical framework is intended as a starting point to understand a common ground for object-oriented methods. It segments object analysis and design into a number of subject areas which can be studied separately. It tries to address the different areas where methods are commonly used today. So far it has focused on concepts used in various existing methods. The technical framework helps assess the extent to which a method supports the various concepts, and should be flexible enough to enable the special features that differentiate each method to be described.

What it is

The technical framework is intended to be a first, high-level identification of the different concepts used in the object-oriented methods that responded to the OMG request for information. It serves as a base for further detailed study in this area.

The definitions of common concepts used in the technical framework are incomplete; different readers will make different interpretations. Additionally, various areas have been described at different levels of detail. This fact does not reflect the relative importance of the areas, but rather reflects the decisions made by the Special Interest Group.

What it is not

The technical framework is not a specification and no method can claim compliance with it. Neither is it intended to be another object model or method.

How it was developed

The technical framework was initially constructed through a process of abstracting common components from 18 method descriptions which were submitted to the Special Interest Group in January 1992. Other methods have since been documented, and more will undoubtedly appear in the future; however the framework has remained unchanged.

Different people have been involved in different parts of the technical framework. Various areas may therefore reflect the authors' opinions rather than that of the entire group. Consensus was attempted within the Special Interest Group, but was not achieved in all cases, due in particular to lack of time and resources.

1.4   THE SURVEY

After completion of the technical framework, it was used as a basis for a survey. The Special Interest Group used the survey to collect information about object analysis and design methods. The survey had two parts:

- A method description asking for a short description of each method written by the method developers in their own terms. These descriptions have been published in *Object Analysis and Design: Description of Methods*.

- A detailed questionnaire based on a technical framework. The results of this work are published in this document.

This approach was adopted because:

- It allowed method developers to provide the information themselves and at their own convenience. This was particularly important because the developers working on object analysis and design methods are spread throughout the world.
- It allowed the effort to be shared in part between the members of the Special Interest Group and with the method developers.
- It ensured that the information was accurate at the time of the survey.

The survey was launched in October 1992 together with the technical framework. OMG made a press announcement and members of the Special Interest Group contacted the developers of many of the methods explaining to them that a survey was being conducted and inviting their participation.

The original timescale for the survey was October to November 1992. By the end of this time about eight survey results had been received and several method developers had asked for and been granted extra time to complete the survey, but many known methods were not being surveyed.

As a result of lack of responses, the Special Interest Group instigated a round of encouraging method developers to respond to the survey.

In two cases, members of the Special Interest group completed the survey for specific methods based on publicly available material. The two methods concerned were Rumbaugh and Wirfs-Brock and in each case the completed survey was sent to the method developer for review. Rumbaugh sent several pages of comments.

The Shlear-Mellor method is not included in the survey at the request of its proponents.

By the end of January 1993, this had produced questionnaire responses from the 16 methods which are surveyed in this document.

1.5   THE METHODS

The table in section 1.6 lists the 16 methods which have been surveyed. The list is in alphabetical order of short and long name.

Note: For complete information about the authors and suppliers, see the appendix.

1.6   PROCESSING THE SURVEY

The criteria for assessing the methods are described in Chapter 2.

The work was done by small teams of people from the Special Interest Group taking responsibility for different areas of the technical framework and assessing all the methods which contribute to that area and writing up their findings for inclusion in this document.

Short name	Method name	Supplier
Booch	Booch Method of Object Analysis and Design	Rational
CCM	Class-Centered Modeling	CASElode Consulting
C/Y/N	Coad, Yourdon, and Nicola: OOA/OOD/OOP	Object International, Inc.
Demeter	Demeter	Northeastern University, Boston
Graham/SOMA	Semantic Object Modeling Approach	BIS Information Systems
IE\O	Information Engineering \with Objects	Texas Instruments
MTD	Marketing to Design	ICL
OBA	Object Behavior Analysis	ParcPlace Systems
Objectory	Objectory	Objective Systems SF AB
OGROUP	OGROUP	Olivetti
OMT	Object-Oriented Modeling and Design	Rumbaugh, General Electric
OOIE	Object-Oriented Information Engineering	James Martin and Co., Intellicorp
SE/OT	Systems Engineering for Object Technology	LBMS
SSADM	SSADM	CCTA
Wirfs-Brock	Responsibility-Driven Design	R Wirfs-Brock
Z++	Z++ Method	Lloyds Register

1.7   FEEDBACK ON THE QUESTIONNAIRE

This work has not only thrown light on the methods and the technical framework, it naturally shows areas where the questionnaire itself was not able to elicit the information that we were seeking.

For this reason, there are several questions which are now recognized by the Special Interest Group as being "incapable of eliciting a meaningful answer"; these questions are explicitly identified in the survey results.

2

Criteria for Assessing the Methods

Many people are as interested in the criteria that were used to handle the survey results as in the results themselves. This is a natural response which recognizes that the state of the art on object analysis and design methods will change year by year, but the criteria could be more stable.

In many ways there are two sets of criteria for assessing methods:

- *Motivational goals*, which explain the different interests of stakeholders in OA&D methods
- *Technical criteria*, which explain how to assess a method

Naturally, when considering the overall value of a method to a particular enterprise, these two sets of criteria become interlinked.

This chapter describes the goals and nongoals that the Special Interest Group adopted in these particular areas.

Note: Part B of the survey is published in *Object Analysis and Design: Description of Methods*, which is a separate volume.

2.1 MOTIVATIONAL GOALS

The Special Interest Group recognizes that the survey of methods was of interest to five groups of people. These groups are:

Developers of methods

Their interests included:

- Taxonomy of commonly agreed (consensus) concepts, techniques, and processes, covered by survey parts D–H, see Chapters 5 to 9

- Combinations of different concepts, techniques, and processes in a method, covered by survey parts D–H, see Chapters 5 through 9
- Overlapping and competing concepts, techniques, and processes, covered by survey parts D–H, see Chapters 5 through 9
- Applicability of combinations of concepts, techniques, and processes to specific application domains, covered by survey part A, see Chapter 3

The question of why the different methods were developed is not covered by the survey.

Selectors of methods (e.g., users)

Their interests included:

- Positioning and coverage of methods, covered by survey parts A (see Chapter 3) and B (see *Object Analysis and Design: Comparison of Methods*)
- Applicability to application domains and development problem domains, covered by survey part A, see *Object Analysis and Design: Description of Methods*
- Organizational impact of using a method, not addressed by survey
- Potential to combine methods, covered by survey parts D–H, see Chapters 5 throught 9

Tools builders

They had technical interests which included:

- Taxonomy of concepts: consensus, similarities, and differences, covered by survey parts D–H, see Chapters 5 through 9
- Taxonomy of techniques: consensus, similarities, and differences, covered by survey parts D–H, see Chapters 5 through 9

They also had marketing interests which included:

- Applicability of the method and market share, covered by survey parts A (see Chapter 3) and B (see *Object Analysis and Design: Description of Methods*)
- Positioning in the life cycles, covered by survey part C, see Chapter 4
- Available tools and integrability, covered by parts D–H, see Chapters 5 through 9
- Mapping to construction and implementation phases, partially covered by part H, see Chapter 9

OMG members

Their interests included:

- Taxonomy of commonly agreed (consensus) concepts, techniques, and processes, covered by survey parts D–H, see Chapters 5 through 9

- Why methods were different, covered by parts A (see Chapter 3) and B (see *Object Analysis and Design: Description of Methods*)
- Impact on the OMG architecture, including the OA&D technical framework, covered by conclusions

Special interest group

At a detailed level the objectives of the Special Interest Group in conducting this survey were:

- To facilitate the uptake of object-oriented technology, which is also an overall OMG objective
- To understand the coverage of existing methods
- To assess the extent to which the existing methods matched the technical framework
- To find the similarities and differences among the various object analysis and design methods
- To avoid the creation of a new "standard" method
- To establish a framework to allow tool development
- To ensure that the Special Interest Group was working with up-to-date information

2.2   TECHNICAL CRITERIA

The questionnaire attempted to assess the complete match between a method and the technical framework. However, it was found that in many areas there was a deficiency in the technical framework, the questionnaire, or the methods descriptions, which precluded support for an effective comparison.

The technical criteria which were found to be effective when assessing the methods were:

- Positioning within the overall technical framework
- Comparison with the terminology and concepts defined in the technical framework

2.3   NONGOALS

The Special Interest Group recognizes that there are a number of legitimate goals that others may expect of a survey such as this, but these are not goals for the Special Interest Group. These were:

- Educating people in the various methods
- Trying to find the "best method"
- Saving effort on method development by sharing experience
- Facilitating the interoperability of object-oriented modeling tools
- Trying to minimize the number of methods to support with tools
- Learning from the experiences of others

Survey Results

3

General Questions

INTRODUCTION

This chapter contains the answers to a set of general questions about object analysis and design methods.

- Availability of documentation (Question A1)
- Coverage of the development process (Question A3)
- Training, consultancy, and tool support (Question A4)
- Commercial availability (Question A5)
- Problem domains in which the method has been used (Question A6)

Note that the answers to survey question A2, which was about the names of the method, are not included in this chapter. The answers to this question were used to structure the whole of this part of the document.

A1   REFERENCES TO YOUR METHOD

Question

In what documents is your method described?

Findings

9 of the methods are described in publicly available books. These books do not always provide a thorough description of the method: some describe a preceding or complementary method, and some describe only portions of the method in question. The following methods appear to be adequately described in publicly available books, papers, and conference proceedings:

Booch

C/Y/N

Graham/SOMA

Objectory

OMT

OOIE

SSADM4

Wirfs-Brock

Z++

6 of the methods are described in publicly available papers, articles, and/or conference proceedings, but a comprehensive book has not yet been published.

One method has provided a reference that is only available when purchasing other services from the authors or company.

Conclusions

A great deal of written material on object analysis and design is available; see *Object Analysis and Design: Description of Methods*, where each specific method description includes a reference list.

Method	Comments
Booch	1 public-domain book
CCM	1 public-domain book (in process) 1 white-paper, 1 reference book
C/Y/N	2 public-domain books plus course notes, a video, and a game
Demeter	Many published papers
Graham/SOMA	1 public-domain book and 1 in-process book 2 papers
IE\O	1 white-paper, 4 relevant public-domain books, 2 internal books not available without other services
MTD	7 internal books not available without other services 1 submission to OMG RFI, several published articles
OBA	1 published article, 1 internal course notebook not available without other services, 2 unpublished books/papers not yet available
Objectory	
OGROUP	1 internal document not available without other services
OMT	1 public-domain book
OOIE	2 public-domain books, 1 course notes, and 2 internal documents not available without other services
SE/OT	2 published articles, 3 manuals not available without other services
SSADM4	10 public-domain books, 4 public-domain manuals, 1 future book
Wirfs-Brock	1 public-domain book
Z++	5 public-domain books

A2   SCOPE OF SUPPORT FOR THE TECHNICAL FRAMEWORK

Question

Which areas of the technical framework do you support with your method?

Indicate the scope of your method in terms of its coverage of each of the subject areas of object analysis and design by deleting those which do not apply to your method.

Object modeling	No coverage	Partial coverage	Comprehensive coverage
Strategic modeling	No coverage	Partial coverage	Comprehensive coverage
Analysis modeling	No coverage	Partial coverage	Comprehensive coverage
Design modeling	No coverage	Partial coverage	Comprehensive coverage
Implementation modeling	No coverage	Partial coverage	Comprehensive coverage

Findings

Reminder: These are unaudited answers, taken without interpretation from the survey responses. We have simply accepted the respondents' ratings.

The table that follows and the table on page 16 use the abbreviations:

n   No coverage

p   Partial coverage

c   Complete coverage

Summary of findings

Responses	C	P	N
Object modeling:	12	3	1
Strategic modeling:	5	4	7
Analysis modeling:	12	3	1
Design modeling:	11	5	0
Implementation modeling:	6	6	4

For several respondents to the survey, the five "subject areas" of object analysis and design were inappropriate for describing the scope of the method. In particular:

- CCM: The technical framework is expressed in terms of Application Analysis and Design, whereas CCM is focused on Class Analysis, Design, and Reuse.
- OMT: There was not a good correspondence between the technical framework's design/implementation modeling subject areas and OMT's stages.

Method	Comments: Object	Strategic	Analysis	Design	Implementation
Booch	c	p	c	c	c
CCM	c	n	p	p	n
C/Y/N	c	c	c	c	c
Demeter	c	n	p	c	c
Graham/SOMA	c	c	c	p (under development)	n (under development)
IE\O	c	c	c	c	c
MTD	p	p	c	p	p
OBA	p	p	c	c	p
Objectory	c	p (under development)	c	c	c
OGROUP	n	n	n	p	n
OMT	c	n	c	c (mismatched)	c (mismatched)
OOIE	c	c	c	c	p
SE/OT	c	n (not OT-specific)	c	c	p
SSADM4	p	c	c	p	p (rest from suppliers)
Wirfs-Brock	c	n	c	c	n
Z++	c	n	p	c	p

Conclusions

This question was inadequate to distinguish the coverage/positioning of the different methods.

1. The "subject area" distinctions made in the technical framework appear to be biased toward a certain style of development, which makes it a bit of a mismatch for certain methods.
2. The meanings of the terms "support," "comprehensive coverage," and "partial coverage" were not explicit, and it is evident that these were interpreted quite differently from respondent to respondent.
3. The question does not reveal whether the strengths of a method lie in methodology/process, technique, or representation, or in some combination of these. A method may be strong in certain of these aspects, and be

compatible with another method that is strong in a different aspect, but comparing them all in one basket sets them up as competitive.

4. The technical framework does not recognize the distinction between re-usable class/domain development and application development, which is an important aspect for some methods.

A3   SUPPORT FOR YOUR METHOD

Question

Is your method supported by:

training	Yes/No
consultancy	Yes/No
tools	Yes/No

Findings

All methods except for OGROUP and IE\O are currently supported by training.

All methods except IE\O are currently supported by consultancy.

10 of the 16 methods are supported by tools to some degree. However, the survey does not ask any questions about the level of support. It also does not address the question of whether the tools are publicly available as products.

Conclusions

It appears that OO methods training is widely available. However, the question does not address whether the training is supported by public courses or on-site training, or perhaps neither. It also does not address the question of who is offering the training.

The survey does not ask for the names of the tools which support each method; any future survey should ask for this.

The survey is not explicit about the definition of "support" for consultancy, training, or tools.

Method	Support for: Training	Consultancy	Tools
Booch	Yes	Yes	Yes
CCM	Yes	Yes	Not Yet
C/Y/N	Yes	Yes	Yes
Demeter	Yes	Yes	Yes
Graham/SOMA	Yes	Yes	Partial
IE\O	No (future)	No (future)	No (future)
MTD	Yes	Yes	Yes

Method	Support for: Training	Consultancy	Tools
OBA	Yes	Yes	Yes
Objectory	Yes	Yes	Yes
OGROUP	No	Yes	No
OMT	Yes	Yes	Yes
OOIE	Yes	Yes	Yes
SE/OT	Yes	Yes	No (future)
SSADM4	Yes	Yes	Yes
Wirfs-Brock	Yes	Yes	No?
Z++	Yes	Yes	No

A4 COMMERCIAL ISSUES

Question

Is your method commercially available?   Yes/No

How many reference sites are there for your method?   _____

Findings

11 of the methods are commercially available.

For those that are commercially available, the number of reference sites varies significantly.

Conclusions

The questions are not explicit in defining "commercially available" or "reference site." One company might say that until they have put in place a large support network for their method, the method is not commercially available, while another might say that the method is available even when it is still being tested with its first users.

Furthermore, a public-domain method (one for which a comprehensive book has been published) may have any number of practitioners, but the respondent will not know how many.

Perhaps the "reference sites" question is more specific to tools that support the method or to training/consultancy customers.

Method	Commercially available?	Number of reference sites
Booch	Yes	2000 (1)
CCM	No (future)	0
C/Y/N	Yes	200 plus
Demeter	Yes	30 plus

Method	Commercially available?	Number of reference sites
Graham/SOMA	No	0
IE\O	No (future)	0
MTD	Yes	3
OBA	Yes	about 10
Objectory	Yes	about 20
OGROUP	No	0
OMT	Yes	?
OOIE	Yes	10 plus
SE/OT	Yes	2
SSADM4	Yes	Many (open method)
Wirfs-Brock	Yes	?
Z++	No	15

Notes about the table

(1) There are more than 2000 licenses for the ROSE tools which support the Booch method.

A5   PROBLEM DOMAINS OF YOUR METHOD

Question

Please list typical problem domains where your method has been used.

Findings

Of the methods surveyed:

13 identified having been used typically in IS domains.

8 identified having been used typically in real-time domains.

4 identified having been used typically in systems software domains (GUI environments, compilers, operating systems).

9 identified having been used typically in CASE Tools development.

2 identified having been used typically in Artificial Intelligence domains.

5 identified having been used typically in Telecommunications domains.

Conclusions

As is evidenced by the responses, OO analysis and design methods are used in a wide range of problem domains.

The question was worded in terms of problem domains in which the method has been used, but many of the responses were more in terms of how the method ·could be used.

Method	Comments
Booch	MIS, telecommunications, manufacturing, defense, CASE tool development, petroleum industry, financial, air traffic control, process control, medical, and more . . .
CCM	Event-driven information systems (e.g., computer-aided emergency dispatching (police/fire/ambulance); ideal for class reuse, as opposed to application design
C/Y/N	Telecommunications, banking, insurance, transportation, government/administration, government/military (including real time), health, manufacturing, utilities, document management, CASE
Demeter	Business model for bank, CASE tool development
Graham/SOMA	CASE tool development, business/enterprise modeling, migrating package to OT, GUI construction, expert systems design
IE\O	Large-scale; client/server, data sharing IS applications
MTD	CASE tool development, operating system user interfaces, systems management, security software, company procedures, applications (~40 systems in all)
OBA	Semiconductor manufacturing, billing systems, reuse library design, resource allocation system
Objectory	Distributed real-time systems, MIS, telecommunications, medical, and more
OGROUP	Software engineering tools, tools for mathematical modeling
OMT	Compilers, graphics, user interfaces, databases, OO languages, CAD systems, simulation, meta-models, control systems
OOIE	Financial, manufacturing (discrete and continuous), health, telecommunications
SE/OT	Financial, retail, payroll/personnel, management information
SSADM4	Large information systems which use conventional DBMS
Wirfs-Brock	All problem domains
Z++	Business information systems, artificial intelligence, communication protocols, reverse engineering, program validation

4

Life Cycle Models

INTRODUCTION

This chapter covers the overall shape of the development process. This is often referred to as the life cycle of the method. We have broken this topic into four main facets of the development process. The questions asked were:

- Do you advocate a particular life cycle model? (Question C1)
- Which iteration strategies are advised by the method? (Question C2)
- Which packaging strategies are advocated by the method? (Question C3)
- Which progression strategy is used by the method? (Question C4)
- What checkpointing strategies are advised by the method? (Question C5)

C1   MODEL TYPE

Questions

C1.1   Do you advocate a particular "life cycle model"?
Yes/No

C1.2   If yes, name and describe this model:
Name _____
Description _____
Ref./Page _____

Findings

2 advocated no life cycle model or did not answer this question [Demeter, OGROUP].

3 advocate any/many life cycle models [IE/O, MTD, Objectory].

4 advocate spiral life cycle models or variants thereof [Graham/SOMA, MTD, OOIE, Wirfs-Brock].

1 advocates incremental (phased-implementation) life cycle model [SE/OT].

3 advocate waterfall life cycle models [SSADM4, Z++, OMT].

1 advocates a dual life cycle model (any life cycle model within either life cycle) [CCM].

3 advocate iterative, incremental prototyping (not phased implementation)—throw-away or evolutionary prototypes [Booch, OBA].

1 advocates a concurrent development model [C/Y/N].

Conclusions

There are many life cycle models named. Because of a lack of definition of terms (e.g., spiral, incremental prototyping), many of these may actually be more alike than their different names suggest. Most methods recognize an incremental, iterative, spiral, concurrent approach.

There is no common understanding in this area; some methods developers mix this question with question C2. Any future survey should merge this question with C2 or be clarified in the technical framework. It may be a question of the form—what stages are used in the various methods would help.

Method	Comments
Booch	Iterative development Iterative, incremental development with a strong emphasis on architecture as a unifying concept. Staged, incremental prototypes leading to final product.
CCM	Dual life cycle model—components and applications Classes and other reusable components have life cycles independent of applications that use them. The technical framework is primarily focused on applications life cycle. CCM supports any life cycle model within either component– or application–life cycles.
C/Y/N	The concurrent development or "baseball" model is managed with time boxes that focus on frequent, tangible working results (e.g., it might be reasonable to move directly from analysis to programming to get early feedback and refinement ideas on problem domain classes).
Demeter	None advocated
Graham/SOMA	Ammonite model A variant of the risk-driven spiral, with additional detail and support for time-box constrained prototyping.

Method	Comments
IE\O	None advocated (Project Manager chooses among rapid prototyping, evolutionary, incremental, spiral, standard waterfall, cascading waterfall.)
MTD	'V' diagram is used to position parts of method; the spiral model is used as an operational life cycle.
OBA	Yes, but currently unnamed Incremental iteration with use of prototyping, both evolutionary (evolving into final product) and rapid (throw-away) prototyping.
Objectory	The process model Independent, interacting processes allowing for waterfall, rapid prototyping, incremental development, or spiral.
OGROUP	No answer
OMT	Unnamed (cascading waterfall) Independent design of each subsystem identified in analysis.
OOIE	Iterative spiral OOIE can be used with most life cycle models. But with executable models even in strategy and analysis stages, OOIE permits extension of the spiral model beyond just the design and implementation stages.
SE/OT	Incremental and evolutionary Each production increment is influenced by the response of end users to earlier increments (but method's life cycle model is tailorable).
SSADM4	SSADM4 structural model Based on the waterfall model.
Wirfs-Brock	Spiral Iterate through requirements specification, design, implementation, testing.
Z++	Formal object-oriented waterfall model Modified waterfall with stages of domain analysis, requirements capture, system analysis, system design, and system implementation.

C2   ITERATION STRATEGY

Questions

C2.1   Which iteration strategy do you advise between cycles and phases (not within a phase)? The table on page 24 lists iteration strategies identified in section 11.2. Please use the table to indicate which iteration strategy you use for your method (answer Yes/No column).

Iteration strategy   *Do you use it?*

Once-only   Yes/No
Evolutionary   Yes/No
Rapid prototyping Yes/No
Incremental   Yes/No

C2.2   Do you use any other iteration strategy for your method?
Yes/No

C2.3   If yes, give your definition for the strategy below:
Strategy name _____
Definition _____
Ref./Page _____

Findings

Responses were received for 14 of the methods:

- All methods but 1 advised the use of the *incremental* iteration strategy.
- All methods but 1 advised the use of the *rapid prototyping* iteration strategy.
- All methods but 1 advised the use of the *evolutionary* iteration strategy.
- Only 6 methods advised the use of once-only development.

Method	Once-only	Evolutionary	Rapid prototyping	Incremental	Other
Booch	No	Yes	Yes	Yes	
CCM	not applicable, but . . . No	Yes	Yes	Yes	
C/Y/N	No	Yes	Yes	Yes	Yes (1)
Demeter	Yes	Yes	Yes	Yes	
Graham/SOMA	No	Yes	Yes	Yes	Yes (2)
IE\O	Yes	Yes	Yes	Yes	Yes (3)
MTD	No	Yes	Yes	Yes	
OBA	No	Yes	Yes	Yes	
Objectory	Yes	Yes	Yes	Yes	
OGROUP	——	——	——	——	
OMT	Yes	Yes	Yes	Yes	
OOIE	Yes	Yes	Yes	Yes	Yes (4)
SE/OT	No	Yes	No	Yes	Yes (5)
SSADM4	Yes	Yes	Yes	No	Yes (6)
Wirfs-Brock	(N/A)				
Z++	No	No	Yes	Yes	

Notes about the table

(1) Concurrent development (or "baseball") model advises that analysis, design, and programming are all performed within a 4 to 8 week time-box, delivering frequent, tangible, working results. In terms of the technical framework, the method appears to apply the "rapid prototyping" iteration strategy in combination with the "non-staged" packaging strategy.

(2) Revolutionary prototyping—a prototype is built and discarded once requirements are agreed upon.

(3) Spiral model—risk-driven spiral, per Boehm, with risk assessment at the start of each phase.

(4) Extended Boehm spiral—extended into strategy and analysis.

(5) Rapid prototyping used within development increment for requirement elicitation, user interface definition, design assessment, etc.

(6) Specification prototyping—prototyping prior to undertaking detailed logical design tasks, to trap errors and ensure feasibility.

Conclusions

We wonder whether the respondents understood that the question was about the strategy for iterating *between development cycles or phases*. The question did *not* address iteration *within* a single phase of the development cycle.

Some respondents proposed that iteration strategy and life cycle model were one and the same.

Some methods, while not advocating a particular life cycle model, have responded to the question since the question asked "Do you use it?" rather than "Is it a part of your method?" Thus, for methods such as CCM and Wirfs-Brock, which do not specify a particular life cycle model or iteration strategy, this question is not applicable.

C3   PACKAGING STRATEGY

Questions

C3.1 Which packaging strategy do you advise? Please indicate which of the following packaging strategies you use in your method (answer Yes/No column).

Strategy	*Do you use it?*
Fixed	Yes/No
Flexible	Yes/No
Nonstaged	Yes/No

C3.2 Do you use any other packaging strategy in your method?
Yes/No

C3.3 If yes, give a description of the strategy below:

Strategy name _____

Description _____

Ref./Page _____

Findings

We received 13 actual responses.

4 methods advocate fixed packaging of development activities into stages but all of them also support flexible packaging. SSADM4 explained what they meant by supporting both flexible and fixed packaging.

12 methods advocate flexible packaging.

7 methods advocate nonstaged development.

6 methods supported both flexible and nonstaged packaging—although all three strategies were intended to be mutually exclusive.

Method	Fixed	Flexible	Nonstaged	Other
Booch	No	Yes	Yes	No
CCM	(not applicable)			
C/Y/N	No	No	Yes	Yes (5)
Demeter	No	Yes	Yes	No
Graham/SOMA	No	Yes	Yes	No
IE\O	No	Yes (1)	No	No
MTD	Yes	Yes	?	Yes (2)
OBA	No	Yes	Yes	No
Objectory	Yes	Yes	?	Yes (3)
OGROUP	No response			
OMT	Yes	Yes	Yes	No
OOIE	No	Yes	No	No
SE/OT	No	Yes	Yes	No
SSADM4	Yes	Yes	No	Yes (4)
Wirfs-Brock	None apparent			
Z++	No	Yes	No	No

Notes about the table

(1) 4 packaging strategies are given as examples.

(2) Object-oriented packaging—each activity creates an instance of a specific group-and-view concept. Development is controlled by a chart showing the causal relationships between these concepts.

(3) Configuration and development cases—objectory has four different configurations; each configuration has predefined development cases and new ones can be defined.

(4) SSADM4 structural model—fixed packaging is defined for those that want it, but flexible packaging is possible since SSADM4 defines the deliverables of each

substage, which allows users to select different techniques to those defined in core SSADM4.

(5) C/Y/N state their packaging strategy is "frequent, tangible working results." This has already been noted under "iteration strategy," where it is more applicable.

Conclusions

All OO methods support either the *nonstaged* packaging or the *flexible* packaging of development activities into stages/phases.

A minority of methods also advocate *fixed* packaging (i.e., a given activity is not always allocated to the same stage in every project that uses the method).

We should have made it clear to the respondents that they should select only one packaging strategy. This issue needs to be clarified in the technical framework.

C4   PROGRESSION STRATEGY

Questions

C4.1   Which progression strategy do you use between phases? Please indicate one of the following:

Strategy	*Do you use it?*
Transformational	Yes/No
Additive	Yes/No

C4.2   Do you use any other progression strategy in your method?
Yes/No

C4.3   If yes, give a description of the strategy below.
Strategy name _____
Description _____
Ref./Page _____

Findings

14 respondents answered this question.

All of them stated their method used additive progression.

6 methods said that transformational progression was also used to some degree. 3 of these (SSADM4, OMT, and Objectory) emphasized that progression is a combination of additive and transformational. 1 method (IE\O) considered that transformation was a "technique" that might be used for some activities. The other method (MTD) did not offer any further explanation.

One respondent (OBA) explained their method was best described as a revisionary progression. OMT made a distinction between transformation (to optimize) and mechanical mapping (to implement).

(CCM's answer was ignored, since they explained it was not really applicable to their method.)

Method	Transformational	Additive	Other
Booch	Yes	Yes	
CCM	not applicable, so . . .		
	Yes	Yes	
C/Y/N	No	Yes	
Demeter	No	Yes	
Graham/SOMA	No	Yes	
IE\O	No (1)	Yes	
MTD	Yes	Yes	
OBA	No	Yes	revisionary (2)
Objectory	Yes	Yes	combination (3)
OGROUP	No response		
OMT	Yes (7)	Yes (7)	map mechanically (7)
OOIE	No	Yes	enactable specifications (8)
SE/OT	No	Yes	
SSADM4	Yes (4)	Yes (5)	hybrid (6)
Wirfs-Brock	None apparent		
Z++	No	Yes	

Notes about the table

(1) IE\O: . . . except there is a transformation from the implementation model into executable code. Also transformation is sometimes a technique used to "add" more objects to the model.

(2) OBA: Revisionary. Progress is made by revising previous results. Previous results are examined in the context of new results, then the previous results may be revised or combined with the new. Most sophisticated abstractions get identified this way.

(3) Objectory: For object models, between different processes, a transformational progression is used; but within a stage the progression is additive. For the use case model, progression is additive.

(4) SSADM4: e.g., LDM to ELHs to ECDs to UPMs; and DFDs to functions. It is additive in the sense that more detail is added to the model as the method progresses.

(5) SSADM4: e.g., RDA results added to LDM; and user interface added to event-entity model. It is not transformational in the sense that the products from one stage have to be transformed before they can be input to the next: they are transformed *during* the next stage.

(6) SSADM4: In common with all methods errors found may necessitate reworking of earlier products or discarding earlier work.

(7) OMT: Progression strategy best described as: Analysis ——(add)——> Design —— (transform) ——> Optimized Design ——(map mechanically) ——> Implementation. Note that System Design is more like the overall structure of the design model than a separate model format.

(8) OOIE supports enactable specifications which are "executable" without code generation.

Conclusions

We were interested to know whether the methods generally transformed their models at some particular point during the development cycle (e.g., an analysis model is transformed into a design model). Non–OO structured methods often use such transformations.

Additive progression is clearly the dominant strategy (although we remain unsure how many respondents realized we were not really concerned about the fact that pretty well every method expects that, within a stage or activity, a model is built by progressive addition and correction).

Only in SSADM4, OMT, Objectory—and possibly IE\O and MTD—does a transformation of the model appear to be a significant activity within the development process. We suggest that SSADM4 is predominantly a transformational method, Objectory and OMT are "hybrid," and the rest are best described as additive methods.

OBA state that their method is "revisionary." While this is probably the case in all methods, it is, perhaps, significant that only OBA choose to emphasize this style of progression.

We would suggest that a future technical framework could include four progression strategies: Additive, Transformation (transforming an extant model), Mapping (creating a new model), and Combination.

C5   CHECKPOINTING STRATEGIES

Questions

C5.1 Which checkpointing strategy (management control strategy between phases and cycles) do you advise? Please indicate which strategy you use in the table below:

Strategy	*Do you use it?*
Rubber-stamp	Yes/No
Management Reviews	Yes/No
Risk-driven	Yes/No

C5.2 Do you use any other checkpointing strategy in your method?
Yes/No

C5.3 If yes, give a description of the strategy below:
Strategy name _____
Description _____
Ref./Page _____

Findings

11 methods have an angle on this subject. (Demeter's answer has been ignored, since they answered "no" to all questions—including "other strategies.")

All methods said they conducted management reviews between the phases or cycles of their method.

9 of these said they also used "risk-driven" checkpoints—i.e., they consciously apply formal risk reduction techniques as the beginning of each new cycle or stage of a project (Boehm's spiral model being the most well-known example of this).

3 methods said that they also used simple "rubber-stamp approval of a stage/go-ahead for next stage."

5 of 16 methods do not appear to have any position on this project management control issue.

Method	Rubber-stamp	Management review	Risk-driven	Other
Booch	No	Yes	Yes	No
CCM	Not applicable			
C/Y/N	Yes (6)	Yes (6)	Yes (6)	model critique (7)
Demeter	No	No	No	No
Graham/SOMA	No	Yes	Yes	time-boxing (1)
IE\O	No	Yes	Yes	internal review (2)
MTD	No	Yes	No	No
OBA	No	Yes	Yes	Holistic goal and objective verification (3)
Objectory	Yes	Yes	Yes	Yes (4)
OGROUP	No response			
OMT	Not addressed by method			
OOIE	No	Yes	No	
SE/OT	No	Yes	Yes	No
SSADM4	Yes	Yes	Yes	No
Wirfs-Brock	(indeterminate)			
Z++	No	Yes	Yes	No

Notes about the table

(1) Graham/SOMA. Time-boxing. Each prototype step is evaluated by an evaluation team at a fixed time reckoned in days elapsed from the start of the time-box.

(2) IE\O. Internal review. The project leader may decide whether to progress to next phase—instead of external management review—probably making use of the method's checking and confirmation techniques.

(3) OBA. Holistic goal and objective verification. When an incremental development strategy is adopted, at the end of each increment we must integrate the new increment and verify that the overall goals and objectives are being adhered to.

(4) Objectory. This is a project management issue. All these strategies are used.

(5) OOIE. End of stage review/planning. Each stage ends in a checkpoint which includes scoping of subsequent projects (or stages), prioritization, cost-benefit analysis. Milestones are used within stages. These are synchronization points for deliverables. Each milestone has predefined quality checks.

(6) C/Y/N. In each case, the checkpointing is "based upon frequent, tangible, working results."

(7) C/Y/N. The model critique checkpoint strategy applies detailed syntax and semantic checks to a class and object model.

Conclusions

OO methods usually recommend management reviews between each stage or cycle of the method, and many methods supplement this with risk reduction techniques between stages or cycles.

Five further checkpointing strategies might be added to our original three:

- Model critique (C/Y/N)—or does this just describe *what* is reviewed?
- Internal review (IE\O)—this is, perhaps, similar to C/Y/N's model critique
- Time-boxing (SOMA)—or is this a specialization of rubber stamping?
- Intrastage milestones (OOIE)—which are, strictly speaking, outside the scope of the original question, but seemed significant enough to mention here
- Objective verification (OBA)—or is this simply a crucial aspect of any internal or external review?

5

Object Modeling

INTRODUCTION

This chapter covers questions on:

• Object structure concepts	(Question D1)
• Object behavior concepts	(Question D2)
• Rule concepts	(Question D3)
• Group and view concepts	(Question D4)
• Deliverables of object modeling	(Question D5)
• Activity types	(Question D6)
• Techniques	(Question D7)
• Technical framework	(Question D8)

The separation of object modeling as a distinct subject area from the other four subject areas (strategic, analysis, design, and implementation modeling) has created some confusion. Some respondents understood object modeling to be a separate subject area from the other four while others understood it to be a common underpinning. Depending on this interpretation they repeated in this section the same replies listed in sections E, F, G, and H, or they split the concepts between them.

The level of detail provided by the answers has enabled us to provide more than one section in this chapter for the above questions. For example, the responses to question D1 are presented in sections D1.1, etc.

One method (OGROUP) does not address object modeling in a generic fashion; therefore its survey response for this question is missing. The following findings and conclusions apply to the remaining 15 methods.

D1   OBJECT STRUCTURE CONCEPTS

D1.1   OBJECT TYPES

Question

Does your method support object types? If yes, does your definition of an object type match the OMG definition (as used in the technical framework)? If your definition does not match, please give your definition.

Findings

All the respondents have a concept corresponding to "object type," with some slight variations from the technical framework definitions.

9 methods use the term "object type," 4 use the term "class," and 2 use the term "entity" (type).

Method	Object types
Booch	Yes
CCM	Yes, uses "class"; needs more specific definition of object type
C/Y/N	Yes, uses "class"
Demeter	Yes, uses different object types to address construction, alternation, and repetition
Graham/SOMA	Yes
IE\O	Yes, uses "encapsulated entity types"
MTD	Yes
OBA	Yes—to the extent that the definition refers to the service interface of objects
Objectory	Yes, but uses a slightly different definition from survey; questions the wording of the concept in the technical framework, e.g., whether "definition" implies supertypes
OMT	Yes, uses "class"
OOIE	Yes
SE/OT	Yes
SSADM4	Yes, uses "entities"
Wirfs-Brock	Yes, uses "class"
Z++	Yes

Conclusions

The terms used in the various methods are not always consistent with the OMG architecture, which assigns specific meanings to three concepts:

- Object type: a definition of some set of object instances with similar behavior. A type is a semantic property.
- Class: an implementation of an object type.
- Object: implying an instantiation of an object type.

It would be helpful if all methods adopted the OMG terminology and recognized the distinction between an object type and a class.

D1.2 ATTRIBUTE TYPES

Question

Does your method support attribute types? If yes, does your definition of an attribute type match the OMG definition (as used in the technical framework)? If your definition does not match, please give your definition.

Findings

9 methods (C/Y/N, Demeter, Graham/SOMA, IE\O, MTD, OOIE, OMT, SE/OT) agreed with the technical framework.

4 methods recognize a separate concept of attribute type, but adopt different approaches or definitions:

- CCM provides a more specific definition: an attribute type is a characteristic of a class that describes a piece of information that instances of the class are responsible for maintaining (examples: the "customer" class has attributes like customer name, customer address)
- Objectory provides separate treatments for:
  — "attribute type": the structure of the data stored in an attribute, i.e., its type
  — "attribute": the unit that holds the value of the data
- OBA distinguishes between different definitions during analysis modeling on the one hand, and design and implementation modeling on the other hand, but does not provide a generic definition for object modeling.
- SSADM4 says: "An attribute is a characteristic of an entity, that is any detail that serves to qualify, identify, classify, quantify, or express the state of an entity. Each attribute describes (is a characteristic of) one and only one entity. An attribute value is the value of an attribute for a given entity occurrence which can only have one such value at a time." Examples of attributes of the entity "Applicant" are "Name," "Date-of-birth," and "Annual income."

Booch does not distinguish attribute types from other classes, but considers them as more general classes that are generally reusable throughout the model (example: name, address, money, . . .).

Finally, Wirfs-Brock does not include attributes explicitly, saying that they are "implied by the specification of class responsibilities and collaborations."

Method	Attribute types
Booch	No, no distinction between attribute types and other classes. Considers them to be more general classes that are reusable throughout the model. Examples are: name, address, money, ...
CCM	Yes, but provides a more specific definition. An attribute type is a characteristic of a class that describes a piece of information that instances of the class are responsible for maintaining (for example, the customer class has attributes like customer name and customer address).
C/Y/N	Yes, uses "attribute."
Demeter	Yes
Graham/SOMA	Yes
IE\O	Yes
MTD	Yes
OBA	Yes, distinguishes between definitions used in analysis modeling vs. definitions used in design and implementation modeling. Does not provide a generic definition for object modeling.
Objectory	Yes, treats attribute types and attributes differently: — attribute type: the structure of the data stored in an attribute, i.e., its type — attribute: the unit that holds the value of the data
OMT	Yes
OOIE	Yes
SE/OT	Yes
SSADM4	Yes, uses "attribute." "An attribute is a characteristic of an entity, that is any detail that serves to qualify, identify, classify, quantify, or express the state of an entity. Each attribute describes (is a characteristic of) one and only one entity. An attribute value is a value of an attribute for a given entity occurrence, which can only have one such value at a time. For example, an entity 'Applicant' has attributes 'name,' 'date of birth,' and 'annual income.'"
Wirfs-Brock	No, not explicitly. They are implied by the specification of class responsibilities and collaborations.
Z++	Yes

Conclusions

There is a general agreement, with few exceptions, about the concept of attribute type. Although several methods use alternate definitions, the fact that they use the same examples (e.g., name) indicates that the differences are more those of terminology than of semantics.

Several methods indicate attribute types are more than nonobject types. For example, Booch distinguishes itself from the others as treating attribute types as classes, while Objectory adds the notion of structure, which is not implied in the OMG architecture definition of a nonobject type.

OMG and OA&D SIG members should note: the OMG object model should either clarify that a nonobject type may include additional structure and semantics beyond what is implied by the CORBA examples (long, short, etc.), or add an explicit concept of "value domain" to add such structure and semantics. This would then explicitly support the richer notion of an attribute type.

D1.3 RELATIONSHIP TYPES

Question

Please indicate whether you use the following concepts in object modeling: association, usage, aggregation, specialization, instantiation. If you have renamed these concepts in your method, please give your name and definition in the alternative name column. Please define any additional relationship types used in your method.

Findings

The following six tables summarize the answers to the questions about which types of relationships are supported in each method. They indicate the alternate name, if any, used by each method for each concept, the existence of comments about the applicability of the concept, and the additional types of relationships included in some methods ("Others" column).

The main findings in the tables are:

- 14 methods support an association relationship.
- 13 methods support a usage relationship.
- 13 methods specifically support an aggregation relationship; 3 of them treat aggregation as a specialization of association.
- All the methods support a specialization relationship, albeit with the different emphases implied by the names they use.
- All the methods support an instantiation relationship.
- 7 methods support other forms of relationship.

Method	Relationship type: Association
Booch	Yes
CCM	Yes
C/Y/N	Yes, uses "object connection"
Demeter	Yes, uses "construction"
Graham/SOMA	Yes

Method	Relationship type: Association
IE\O	Yes, uses "semantic relationship"
MTD	Yes, but uses specific names
OBA	Yes
Objectory	Yes, uses "acquaintance"
OMT	Yes, uses "relationship" but makes extra distinctions: — binary, ternary, or higher order associations — involuted recursive associations — ordered associations — associations "modeled as classes" — "qualified associations"
OOIE	Yes
SE/OT	Yes, uses "relationship"
SSADM4	Yes, uses "named relationship"
Wirfs-Brock	No: association is implicit in the responsibilities
Z++	Yes

Method	Relationship type: Usage
Booch	Yes
CCM	Yes
C/Y/N	Yes, uses "message"
Demeter	Yes
Graham/SOMA	Yes
IE\O	Yes, uses "collaboration"
MTD	Yes
OBA	Yes
Objectory	Yes, uses "communication"
OMT	No, but this is similar to "event flow"
OOIE	Not supported in the basic object relationship diagram, but can be represented by an association, and has an equivalent in the optional object communication diagram
SE/OT	Yes, uses "collaboration"
SSADM4	Yes
Wirfs-Brock	Yes
Z++	Yes, uses "composition/vertical inheritance"

Method	Relationship type: Aggregation
Booch	Yes
CCM	Treats it as a special case of association
C/Y/N	Yes, uses "whole-part" in object discovery and in the OOA/OOD model organization. There are three kinds of "whole-part": assembly and parts, container and contents, and collection and members.
Demeter	Yes, uses "construction" (treats aggregation as a special case of association)
Graham/SOMA	Yes, uses "composition"
IE\O	Yes, uses "containment"
MTD	Yes, uses "contains," "has parts" (specializations of aggregation)
OBA	Yes
Objectory	Yes, uses "consists of" (treats aggregation as a special case of association)
OMT	Yes, uses aggregation—a specialization of association
OOIE	Yes, uses "composition"
SE/OT	Yes
SSADM4	Yes
Wirfs-Brock	No, implicit in the relationships
Z++	Yes

Method	Relationship type: Specialization
Booch	Yes
CCM	Yes, uses "subclassification"
C/Y/N	Yes, uses "generalization-specialization (gen-spec)"
Demeter	Yes, uses "inheritance"
Graham/SOMA	Yes, uses "inheritance/classification (a kind of)"
IE\O	Yes, uses "inheritance"
MTD	Yes, uses "ISA"
OBA	Yes
Objectory	Yes, uses "inheritance"
OMT	Yes, uses "generalization"
OOIE	Yes, uses "specialization/generalization"
SE/OT	Yes, uses "subtype/supertype"
SSADM4	Yes, uses "supertype/subtype"
Wirfs-Brock	Yes, uses "inheritance"
Z++	Yes

Method	Relationship type: Instantiation
Booch	Yes
CCM	Yes
C/Y/N	Yes, uses class-and-object symbol (represents a class and the objects in that class)
Demeter	Yes
Graham/SOMA	Yes, uses "inheritance/classification (is a)"
IE\O	Yes, uses "entity creation"; not represented in diagrams as an association.
MTD	Yes
OBA	Yes
Objectory	No (implicit)
OMT	Yes
OOIE	Yes
SE/OT	Yes
SSADM4	Yes
Wirfs-Brock	Yes, but does not represent it explicitly
Z++	Yes

Method	Relationship type: Others
Booch	
CCM	
C/Y/N	
Demeter	
Graham/SOMA	Relationship Fuzzy inheritance
IE\O	Partitioning of subclasses Subject area association
MTD	Contains Has part (specializations of aggregation)
OBA	Composition (form of aggregation) All relationships are defined in terms of contracts
Objectory	Association (not what technical framework calls association)
OMT	Link: an instance of an association Homomorphism: a relation between two associations

Method	Relationship type: Others
OOIE	
SE/OT	
SSADM4	
Wirfs-Brock	Has-knowledge-of Is-analogous-to Depends-on (used informally)
Z++	Conformant inheritance

Conclusions

The different kinds of relationships included in the technical framework seem appropriate since most methods have corresponding concepts. However, the terminology in this area is not standardized, and the number of additional distinctions offered by the respondents indicate a need to define the concepts more precisely.

The technical framework's definition of "instantiation" is confusing because it seems to refer to a specific point in time (creation of an instance of a class) rather than to the static relationship between the instance and its object type. The names used by Graham/SOMA and IE\O (see tables on pages 38 to 41) reflect this confusion.

Not all methods define relationships as bidirectional. Some (like Booch) define only unidirectional relationships, while OMT allows more than two objects to be connected by an association relationship.

D2 OBJECT BEHAVIORAL CONCEPTS

Question

The table below lists object behavioral concepts identified in section 12.3.5. You should read the section before answering this question.

D2.1   Please use the table to indicate whether you use the concept in object modeling (answer Yes/No column).

If you have renamed this concept in your method, please give your name in the alternative name column and your definition of this concept.

Concept	Do you use it?	Alternative name or term
Operation	Yes/No	
Method	Yes/No	
Event	Yes/No	

Concept	*Do you use it?*	*Alternative name or term*
Internal event	Yes/No·	
External event	Yes/No	
State	Yes/No	
Transition	Yes/No	
Message	Yes/No	
Request	Yes/No	

D2.2 Does your method use alternative definitions and/or other object behavioral concepts?

Yes/No

D2.3 If yes, give your definition for these using the following template:

Concept _____

Definition _____

How it is used _____

Ref./Page _____

Findings

The following three tables summarize the coverage of the nine behavior concepts defined in the technical framework.

Almost all methods (but not MTD and Wirfs-Brock) include Operation, Method, Event State, and Transition. However, terminology and semantics vary, and several methods add other concepts, or specialize these concepts into multiple ones.

There is evidence that when a method does not distinguish between two concepts, the responses are inconsistent: some respondents say that they address both concepts (with a note saying that they treat them the same way) while others will answer "yes" to one and "no" to the others.

Most methods have a model of the relationship between these behavioral concepts that is different from that expressed in the technical framework (see diagram in section 12.3.5).

Multiple respondents redefined the concept of "event" to indicate that it does not necessarily correspond to a state change.

Conclusions

All the methods support a set of behavioral concepts.

Although there are a core of common concepts (operation, method, event, state, and transition), the terminology of behavioral concepts is more diverse than for object structure concepts.

Since the various behavioral concepts are highly interrelated, but the relationships are different according to the method, asking each respondent to explicitly define the relationships between the behavioral concepts would have been helpful.

The technical framework's definition of an event is too limiting and needs to change.

We are not convinced that:

- the distinction between message and request is well accepted;
- the distinction between internal and external event is well accepted.

Demeter's response prompts the question: are any of these behavioral concepts best represented by regular object types?

Method	Operation	Method	Message	Request
Booch	Yes	Yes	Yes	Yes
CCM	Yes	Yes	Yes, "message event"	Yes, "request event"
C/Y/N	Yes, "service"	Yes, "method" or "function"	Yes	Yes
Demeter	Yes, "interface"	Yes, "function"	Yes, modeled as objects	Yes, "function call"
Graham/SOMA	Yes, "method"	Yes, "method body"	Yes	Yes, treated as message
IE\O	Yes, "operation"	Yes, with broader definition	Different definition	Yes
MTD	Yes, "action"	Yes	No	No
OBA	Yes, "service"	Yes, "method"	Yes	Yes, "contract"
Objectory	Yes, different definition	Yes, "implementation of operation"	Yes, "stimuli"	Yes, "stimuli"
OMT	Yes	Yes	No	No, but has "invocation of operations"
OOIE	Yes	Yes	Yes	Yes
SE/OT	Yes	Yes, "operation code"	Yes	Yes
SSADM4	Yes, "effect"	Yes but	Yes	Yes, external or internal
Wirfs-Brock	Yes, "method" or "signature"	No, treated as operation	No, same as request	Yes, "message"
Z++	Yes	Yes	Yes	Yes

Method	State	Transition	Event	Internal event	External event
Booch	Yes	Yes	Yes	Yes	No
CCM	Yes	Yes	Yes, different definition	Yes	Yes
C/Y/N	Yes	Yes	Yes	Yes	Yes
Demeter	Yes, modeled as objects	Yes, modeled as method	Yes, modeled as objects	Yes, modeled as objects	Yes, modeled as objects
Graham/ SOMA	Yes	Yes	Yes	Yes, treated as event	Yes, treated as event
IE\O	Yes, but different definition	Yes	Yes, but not limited to state changes	Yes	Yes
MTD	Yes	No	Yes	No	No
OBA	Yes	Yes	Yes, "script"	Yes	Yes
Objectory	Yes	Yes, "operation path"	Yes, "stimuli"	Yes, "stimuli"	Yes, "stimuli"
OMT	Yes, can have substates	Yes, caused by an event	Yes, but . . .	No	No, but . . .
OOIE	Yes	Yes	Yes	Yes, 3 types	Yes
SE/OT	Yes	Yes	Yes	No	Yes
SSADM4	Yes	Yes	Yes	No, but . . .	Yes, treated as event
Wirfs-Brock	No	No	No	No	No
Z++	Yes	Yes	Yes	Yes, "spontaneous internal action"	Yes

Method	Others
Booch	
CCM	More special forms of event (e.g., message event, request event)
C/Y/N	Three categories of behavior: event-response, object life history (state-dependent behavior), and basic capabilities that all objects need (specify once, then inherit—extend only when necessary)
Demeter	Propagation pattern
Graham/SOMA	
IE\O	Event, method, message (different definitions)
MTD	
OBA	
Objectory	
OMT	Propagation Delegation
OOIE	Subtyping and composition of behavioral concepts
SE/OT	Command and Query Common event
SSADM4	Additional behavioral concepts can be found in book
Wirfs-Brock	
Z++	

D3 RULE CONCEPTS

Question

The table below lists rule concepts identified in section 12.3.6. You should read the section before answering this question.

D3.1 Please use the table to indicate whether you use the concept in object modeling (answer Yes/No column).

If you have renamed this concept in your method, please give your name in the alternative name column and your definition of this concept.

Concept	Do you use it?	Alternative name or term
Constraint	Yes/No	
Assertion	Yes/No	

D3.2 Does your method use alternative definitions and/or other rule concepts in object modeling?

Yes/No

D3.3 If yes, give your definition for these using the following template:

Concept _____

Definition _____

How it is used _____

Ref./Page _____

Findings

11 methods include both constraints and assertions although there is a variety of different terminology used. Exceptions are:

- Booch and MTD have constraints but no assertions.
- Objectory, Wirfs-Brock, and Z++ have neither.

4 methods have the concepts of precondition, invariant, and postcondition. However, some treat them as constraints (C/Y/N) while others treat them as assertions (Graham/SOMA, IE\O, OMT, SE/OT).

Some methods make many more distinctions. For example, OOIE defines structural (static) and behavior (dynamic) rules while SSADM4 defines specific terms for several forms of constraint and assertion.

OMT considers assertions to be an implementation concept, not an object modeling concept.

Conclusions

Precondition, postcondition, and invariant rules are used in several methods and could be included in the technical framework.

The survey responses showed different interpretations of the terms "constraint" and "assertion." Some used assertion to mean a statement of truth or derivation of some information from other information, while others used the term in the sense of a restriction.

The technical framework needs strengthening. The technical framework and survey questions did not indicate whether cardinality and optionality of relationships, or the definition of a domain for the values of an attribute, constituted a constraint. In retrospect, this should be made clear, and the degree of support for such constraints should be sought (either in this section or in previous ones).

In general, the technical framework implied to some respondents a narrow definition of what rules could be about, because rules can apply to other entities than objects: operations, sets of objects, transitions, relationships, etc. It was also not sufficiently precise in its definitions.

The technical framework does not distinguish between different scopes of constraint; for example, local or global, internal or external.

Method	Constraint	Assertion
Booch	Yes	No
CCM	Yes	Yes
C/Y/N	Yes, uses "attribute constraint," service precondition	Yes, uses "service specifications"
Demeter	Yes, uses "object graph axioms"	Yes, described by method
Graham/SOMA	Yes	Yes, uses "precondition, postcondition, and invariant condition"
IE\O	Yes, uses "integrity constraint or permitted value"	Yes uses "precondition, derivation rule, postcondition, activation rule"
MTD	Yes	No
OBA	Yes, uses "object states"	Yes, uses "object state definition"
Objectory	No	No
OMT	Yes, uses "functional relationship between entities(= object, class, attribute, link, or association) of an object model"	Yes, uses "precondition, post-condition"
OOIE	Yes, uses "integrity(structure), precondition(behavior)"	Yes, uses "derivation (structure), trigger (behavior)"
SE/OT	Yes	Yes, uses "type invariant, precondition, postcondition"
SSADM4	Yes, uses "relationship optionality and cardinality, attribute optionality and validity range, integrity tests in update and inquiry processes, control errors in input data streams, dialogue dependent errors in dialogue definitions"	Yes, same comments as for constraints
Wirfs-Brock	No	No
Z++	No	No

Method	Other rule concepts or alternative definitions
Booch	
CCM	No, at least not explicitly.
C/Y/N	No.
Demeter	Yes, Path Constraints.
Graham/SOMA	Concept: Rule Set/Rule Definition: A finite set of IF/THEN statements in (loosely) Horn Clause form together with a statement of how the rule set behaves under inference (e.g., forward, backward, opportunistic). A rule is a rule set with one member. Used to specify requirements, to simulate and analyze a system. In logical design, used to generate assertions and constraints. Rules capture higher order constructs than constraints and global system behavior. Rules are inherited by both instances and classes and may be overridden or added to.
IE\O	Yes, precondition, activation rule, local integrity constraints.
MTD	No.
OBA	Yes.
Objectory	No.
OMT	Yes, condition = guard on a transition; derived object, link, and attribute; invariant.
OOIE	Yes, 16 rule types—most significantly structural and behavioral rules.
SE/OT	Yes, type invariant; precondition; postcondition.
SSADM4	Yes, constraints and assertions.
Wirfs-Brock	No.
Z++	No.

D4   GROUP AND VIEW CONCEPTS

D4.1 DIAGRAMS

Question

Does your method include any diagrams? If yes, please give descriptions.

Findings

There are anywhere from one to 15 different diagram types included in a method. Because it is impossible, in the current status of imprecise definitions, to ascertain whether two diagrams contain the same information or not, it is impossible to ascertain how many different diagrams have been mentioned in total by the respondents.

There is some inconsistency in how the respondents understood the question. For instance, OMT mentions only one diagram (object model) because other diagrams are not part of "object modeling" but belong to other areas (e.g., analysis modeling). Other respondents seem to have included here all the diagrams their method supports.

The types of diagrams that appear the most often, presumably with closely related semantic contents, are:

- object models (= static view, etc.)
- state diagrams (= life cycle models, dynamic model, etc.)

At the same time, several diagrams capture multiple concepts. For instance, diagrams representing behavior may capture both states and events, while object modeling diagrams may capture both specialization and association. The grouping of concepts into diagrams varies widely from method to method.

Conclusions

The separation of object modeling as a distinct subject area from the other four (strategy, analysis, design, and implementation) has created some confusion in this section.

The technical framework fails to distinguish between two categories of diagram:

- diagrams that actually become part of the system's analysis or design documentation
- diagrams presented onscreen to help an analyst or designer navigate the rest of the model (e.g., by an object browser)

It is hard to identify commonality and discrepancies between methods because of the large number of different diagrams encountered, the fact that each diagram tends to describe multiple concepts at the same time, and the lack of a precise and accepted terminology. A suggestion for further work, which would require significant study of each method, would consist of creating a mapping between the diagrams and the concepts, in order to clearly identify the nature of each diagram type. It would then be possible to determine whether or not diagram X of method A contains the same type of information as diagram Y of method B.

Such an explicit mapping would also help identify any concepts that are not represented in any diagrams, as well as concepts that are represented in several diagrams which, therefore, must be maintained in a consistent state by any tool that automates the creation of these diagrams.

Methods	Diagrams
Booch	Yes; uses "class diagram, object diagram, state diagram, interaction diagram, and category diagram"
CCM	Yes; uses "class and information diagram; class and event diagram; class events and operations diagram; class, events, operations, and methods diagram; method behavior diagram; transition, methods, and event diagram; timing diagram"
C/Y/N	Yes; uses "class and object model (multiple layer OOA/OOD model)"
Demeter	Yes; uses "semi-class dictionary graph, partial class dictionary graph, class dictionary graph, class dictionary and propagation graph"
Graham/SOMA	Yes; uses "class icon, instance icon, classification structure, composition structure, layer, use structure, and association diagram"
IE\O	Yes; uses "object model diagram, object model browser, collaboration diagram, component manager and entity life cycle diagram"
MTD	Yes; uses "IsA and whole-part model"
OBA	Yes; uses "contract diagram, hierarchy diagram, object-level dynamic model diagrams, and system level dynamic model diagram"
Objectory	Yes; uses "views, interaction diagram, and state transition diagram"
OMT	Yes; uses "object model, event model, and function model"
OOIE	Yes; uses "object relationship diagram, event diagram, object state transition diagram, object flow diagram, and object communication diagram"
SE/OT	Yes, uses "static view (also known as object relationship diagram), dynamic view (parallel state chart), collaboration diagram, and usage diagram"
SSADM4	Yes; uses "context diagram, document flow diagram, resource flow diagram, data flow diagram, logical data structure, entity life histories, effect correspondence diagram, inquiry access paths, update process model, inquiry process model, dialogue level structure, IO\E structure diagram, menu structure, specific function models, and physical data model"
Wirfs-Brock	Yes; uses "hierarchy graph, collaboration graphs, and Venn diagrams"
Z++	Yes; uses "usage diagram, object model diagram, state chart, entity life history, and data flow diagram"

D4.2 SCHEMA

Question

Does your method include any schema concepts? If yes, please give your definitions.

Findings

There are anywhere from 0 to 5 constructs submitted in answer to this question. Their names, and presumably their semantics, vary widely according to the interpretation given by the respondents to the question.

Two respondents (OBA and OMT) explicitly indicated that there was an overlap between what the technical framework calls schema vs. architecture.

Booch answered "no" but may have been misled by the question since his book includes subsystem diagrams, which other authors understood to be types of schemas.

The notion of subsystem (also called "module" or "package") is the only common concept that can be recognized among a number of different methods (IE\O, Objectory, OMT, Wirfs-Brock). The same concept might be included in others under a less recognizable name.

Conclusions

The definition of a "schema" in the technical framework needs considerable improvement, as shown by the confusion experienced by the respondents. Methodologists do not differentiate between schema and architecture: both are useful groupings of objects to them. It is even possible that schema and architecture concepts should be merged, or at least that the concept of a subsystem be specifically identified in one place (e.g., under architecture) to remove the confusion about what kind of concept a subsystem is according to the technical framework.

Method	Schema
Booch	No
CCM	No, but "some characteristics of CCM may apply but not as defined in the survey framework which presupposes the use of a set of objects"
C/Y/N	Yes, uses "pattern": a grouping of classes and objects which can be applied in more than one problem domain
Demeter	Yes, uses "semi-class dictionary graph"
Graham/SOMA	Yes, uses "layer"

Method	Schema
IE\O	Yes, uses "subject area, system and subsystems, reusable component, (load)module and component library"
MTD	Yes, uses "list of object types"
OBA	see response to question D4.3
Objectory	Yes, uses "package"
OMT	Yes, uses "module and sheet"
OOIE	Yes, uses "event and object relationship diagrams as schemas"
SE/OT	Yes, uses "design schema"
SSADM4	Yes, uses "specific function model and physical data model"
Wirfs-Brock	Yes, uses "class cards, subsystem cards, class specification, subsystem specification, and contract specification"
Z++	Yes, uses "specification module"

D4.3 ARCHITECTURE

Question

Does your method include any architecture concept? If yes, give your definition.

Findings

Three methods (Aranow, OOIE, Z++) do not address architecture. The others mention 1 to 4 architectural concepts.

3 methods mention the concept of "component": Demeter, MTD, Wirfs-Brock. Demeter and MTD mention "component" as an architecture concept, while OBA, OMT, and Wirfs-Brock mention "subsystem."

5 methods mention either a concept which is explicitly named an architecture, or a concept of layers which corresponds to one's intuitive idea of an architectural concept: SSADM4, IE\O, Graham/SOMA, Objectory, SE/OT.

Conclusions

The findings, combined with those of section D4.2, indicate that the notion of a subsystem is widespread but that the technical framework does not make it clear whether the concept of a subsystem belongs under schema or architecture.

Method	Architecture
Booch	Yes, uses "category"
CCM	No
C/Y/N	Yes, uses the "class and object model and its multiple components"
Demeter	Yes, uses "component"
Graham/SOMA	Yes, uses "layer" as in question D4.2
IE\O	Yes; uses "strategic architecture, area (business area, design area, and implementation area), system design standards, system design requirements/acceptance criteria"
MTD	Yes, uses "component"
OBA	Yes, uses "subsystem"
Objectory	Yes, uses "layers"
OMT	Yes, uses "subsystem"
OOIE	No
SE/OT	Yes, uses "three-layer architecture model"
SSADM4	Yes, uses "three schema architecture and universal function model"
Wirfs-Brock	Yes, "subsystem, component, framework, and application"
Z++	No

D4.4 QUALITY

Question

Does your method include any quality concepts? If yes, give your definitions.

Findings

4 methods (CCM, Booch, OMT, and Wirfs-Brock) answered "no" to this question.

Among the positive responses, two different kinds of quality concepts were mentioned:

- Concepts related to the quality of the system or application under development, for instance performance (or response time), resource utilization, reliability, security, etc.
- Concepts related to the quality of the software engineering process, for instance completeness (OOIE), metrics of the specification structure (Z++), potential for change (MTD).

Two methods (OBA and SSADM4) refer to quality templates (e.g., OBA refers to Tom Gilb's), quality criteria, or software quality assurance without giving further details.

Four methods (C/Y/N, MTD, OOIE, and SE/OT) list specific qualities.

Conclusions

The disparity in the responses makes it hard to draw conclusions. For instance, it may indicate differences of style, maturity, or underlying software engineering process in the methods.

The technical framework should clearly distinguish between the quality of the process and the quality of the product as different concepts (in a way similar to the distinction between validation and verification, or the difference between conformance and compliance). It should also define the relationship between quality and metrics.

Method	Quality
Booch	No
CCM	No; not explicitly and not as defined in the survey framework.
C/Y/N	Yes, uses "quality requirements" which specify reliability, availability, and other quantifiable and measurable requirements. These requirements have specific scope (object, class, scenario, or system).
Demeter	Yes, uses "conformance, use-cases"
Graham/SOMA	Yes, uses "class interfaces to specify the contract and test which must be passed"
IE\O	Yes, addressed using a number of techniques and activities and automatic checking by CASE tool
MTD	Yes, uses "availability, usability (per ISO 9241), performance, security, and potential for change"
OBA	Yes, uses "quality templates"
Objectory	Yes, uses "software quality assurance (multiple activities)"
OMT	No
OOIE	Yes, uses "completeness checking, correctness checking, stability analysis, and model animation"
SE/OT	Yes, uses "nonfunctional attributes (for example, response time, resource utilization, reliability, and environment compatibility)"
SSADM4	Yes, uses "quality criteria"
Wirfs-Brock	No
Z++	Yes, uses "metrics of specification structure"

D4.5   OTHER GROUPS AND VIEWS

Question

Does your method identify any other group and view concepts?

Findings

11 methods list no other groups and view concepts.

SSADM4 says "no quick answer possible" and indicates that there is a difference in how the concepts are organized in the method and the technical framework.

Demeter mentions "propagation directives" and "partial class directory graph." It is possible that these additional concepts would fall under the architecture or schema categories if these were better defined.

Similarly, Graham/SOMA defines the "link between layer interfaces and the internal object interfaces" as an additional concept. This might well fall under architecture too.

Conclusions

An "other groups and views" section is clearly only a way to capture concepts proposed by some methodologists which do not immediately fit in one of the categories of the technical framework. In this case, it does not seem that the technical framework omitted one or more additional concepts, but rather that it provided a definition of schemas and architecture that did not enable the respondents to confidently include their additional concepts into either section.

Method	Other groups and views
Booch	No
CCM	No, but "could use event streams"
C/Y/N	Yes, uses "layer": a mechanism for controlling how much one sees at a time in a class and object model
Demeter	Yes, uses "propagation directive and partial class dictionary graph"
Graham/SOMA	Yes, uses "concepts (implemented as link) and definitions (connects layer interface to internal object interface)
IE\O	No
MTD	No
OBA	No
Objectory	Yes, uses "layers"
OMT	No
OOIE	No
SE/OT	No
SSADM4	No (no quick answer possible)
Wirfs-Brock	No
Z++	No

D5   DELIVERABLES OF OBJECT MODELING

Question

Does your method describe generic deliverables resulting from object modeling? If yes, describe these deliverables (including their use).

Findings

Of the methods surveyed, 10 have generic deliverables, 4 only have phase-specific deliverables.

Most methods include both graphical representations and textual descriptions.

Conclusions

The methods which have generic deliverables seem to have similar diagrams, usually including an object relationship diagram.

The survey question said "Does your method *describe generic deliverables resulting from object modeling*?" This created ambiguity and the replies cannot be compared because they correspond to different interpretations. For instance, some people referred back to all their diagrams, others limited their answers to additional components.

Method	Deliverables
Booch	Yes, "class diagrams," "class specifications"
CCM	Yes, in terms of formats, no in terms of deliverables that must be produced
C/Y/N	Yes, the multilayer, multicomponent class and object model, with supporting text
Demeter	Yes, "propagation pattern" (pps), "class dictionary" (cds), "growth plan" (gps)
Graham/SOMA	Yes, "layer descriptions," "class descriptions," " classification structure diagrams," "composition structure diagrams," "use structure diagrams," and "association diagrams" (ER models) plus annotations. Walkthrough reports. Prototypes. Outline project plans.
IE\O	No, deliverables of each logical stage appear in subsequent sections of this survey
MTD	No, object modeling is used as a tool in analysis and design modeling
OBA	No
Objectory	No
OMT	Yes, "object model" = object model diagram + data dictionary

Method	Deliverables
OOIE	Yes, "object relationship diagram," "event diagram," "object state diagram," "business rules"
SE/OT	Yes, "static view," "object type definition," "dynamic view"
SSADM4	Yes, see D4.1
Wirfs-Brock	Yes, diagrams and schemata in D4.1
Z++	Yes, "class, association, and module descriptions"

D6   ACTIVITIES

Question

Does your method describe a process for generic object modeling? Does it cover the following activities: discover, identify, organize, formalize, review and inspect, feedback/refine, agree? If you have renamed this activity in your method, please give your name and provide your definition.

Does your method use other activities in object modeling? If yes, give a definition of these, and how they are used.

Does your method define entry, exit, and evaluation criteria for the different activities?

Findings

The next four tables summarize the answers to this question.

13 methods include process descriptions for generic object modeling.

As shown in the second table, most of the activities described in the technical framework are supported by most of the methods.

The third table shows that 8 of the methods support other techniques.

The last table shows patchy support for defined entry and exit criteria.

Conclusions

Most methods include most of the activities listed in the technical framework, sometimes using different terminology and with a few additions. But the activities named in the technical framework were, perhaps, too general to promote an interesting response.

It would be interesting to find out how the various entry, exit, and evaluation criteria of the various methods are expressed in the methods that include them.

Method	Process described
Booch	Yes
CCM	No
C/Y/N	Yes
Demeter	Yes
Graham/SOMA	Yes
IE\O	Yes, but not in detail
MTD	Yes
OBA	Yes
Objectory	Concepts only
OMT	Yes
OOIE	Yes
SE/OT	Yes
SSADM4	Yes
Wirfs-Brock	Yes
Z++	Yes

Method	Discover	Identify	Organize	Formalize	Review and inspect	Feedback/refine	Agree
Booch	Yes	Yes	Yes	No	Yes	Yes	Yes
CCM							
C/Y/N	Yes	Yes	Yes	Yes	Yes	Yes	Yes
Demeter	Yes	Yes	Yes	Yes	Yes	Yes	Yes
Graham/SOMA	Yes, problem identification	Yes, analysis and design	Yes, analysis and design	Yes, analysis and design	Yes, evaluation/testing	Yes, evaluation/testing/prototyping	Yes, evaluation/testing/prototyping
IE\O							
MTD	Yes	Yes	Yes	Yes	Yes	Yes	Yes
OBA	Yes	Yes	Yes	Yes	Yes	Yes	Yes
Objectory	No	Yes, find	Yes, structure	Yes, describe	Yes, review	No	No
OMT	No?	Yes	Yes	Yes	Yes	Yes	No
OOIE	Yes, gather information	Yes, classify	Yes, classify	Yes, classify	Yes, confirm	Yes	Yes
SE/OT	Yes	Yes	Yes	Yes	Yes, review	Yes, review rework	Yes
SSADM4	Yes	Yes	Yes	Yes	Yes	Yes	Yes
Wirfs-Brock	Not formally	Not formally	Not formally	Not formally	Not formally	Not formally	Not formally
Z++	No	Yes	Yes	Yes	No	No	No

Method	Other activities
Booch	No
CCM	
C/Y/N	Yes: — Find classes and objects — Identify structure—generalization-specialization — Identify structure—whole-part — Identify subjects — Define attributes — Define services
Demeter	Yes, optimize.
Graham/SOMA	No
IE\O	Yes, object modeling is not broken down into nine separate activities, but details vary according to which techniques are used.
MTD	Yes, evaluation of object models with uses.
OBA	Yes, measure.
Objectory	Yes, assigning behavior.
OMT	Yes, add operations (from functional and dynamic models), group classes into sheets and modules.
OOIE	No
SE/OT	Yes, analyze.
SSADM4	No quick answer possible.
Wirfs-Brock	No
Z++	No

Method	Entry criteria	Exit criteria	Evaluation criteria
Booch	No	Yes	Yes
CCM	No	No	No
C/Y/N	No	No, but Yes for product completion	Yes
Demeter	Yes	Yes	Yes
Graham/SOMA	No	No	No
IE\O	No	No	No
MTD	Yes	Yes	Yes
OBA	Yes	Yes	Yes
Objectory	Yes	Yes	Yes
OMT	No	No	No
OOIE	Yes	Yes	Yes
SE/OT	Yes	Yes	No

Method	Entry criteria	Exit criteria	Evaluation criteria
SSADM4	Yes	Yes	Yes
Wirfs-Brock	No	No	No
Z++	No	Yes	Yes

D7   TECHNIQUES

Question

Which of the following techniques do you describe in your method for object modeling: interviewing, feedback sessions, facilitated group sessions, diagramming, current systems analysis, completeness/consistency checking, stability analysis?

Does your method describe any other techniques for use in object modeling? If yes, give a description (including how they are used).

Findings

The next two tables summarize the answers to this question.

The number of methods using each technique is outlined below:

Technique	No. of methods using it
Interviewing	9
Feedback sessions	7
Facilitated workgroup sessions	7
Diagramming	13
Current systems analysis	7
Completeness, consistency checking	9
Stability analysis	4

The survey questions did not indicate how literally the question should be interpreted. For instance, some methods may use interviewing even if they do not explicitly mention it in their method description.

Several additional techniques were identified, including:

- First-hand observation
- Prototyping
- Playacting
- CRC cards

Conclusions

The current findings must be seen as provisional and indicative. More work is required in this area to provide a definitive list of techniques, and to understand how the methods use them.

Method	Interviewing	Feedback session	Facilitated group sessions	Diagramming	Current systems analysis	Completeness, consistency checking	Stability analysis
Booch	Yes	Yes	No	Yes	Yes	Yes	Yes
CCM	Irrelevant because CCM is a set of diagramming techniques, not a methodology						
C/Y/N	Yes	Yes	Yes	Yes	No	Yes	Yes
Demeter	No	No	No	Yes	Yes	Yes	Yes
Graham/SOMA	Yes	Yes	Yes	Yes	Yes	No	No
IE\O	Yes	Yes	Yes	Yes	Yes	Yes	Yes
MTD	Yes	Yes	Yes	Yes	No	Yes	No
OBA	Yes	Yes	Yes	Yes	Yes	Yes	No
Objectory	No	No	No	Yes	No	No	No
OMT	No	No	No	Yes	No	Yes	No
OOIE	Yes	Yes	Yes	Yes	Yes	Yes	Yes
SE/OT	Yes	No	Yes	Yes	No	Yes	No
SSADM4	Yes	Not specified	Not specified	Yes	Yes	Yes	No
Wirfs-Brock	None formally	None formally	None formally	Yes	None formally	None formally	None formally
Z++	No	No	No	No	No	No	No

Method	Other techniques
Booch	None
CCM	None
C/Y/N	Reading (to gain domain understanding, insights, and scope) First-hand observation Checking previous results (look for reuse opportunities) Prototyping Playacting
Demeter	Unspecified additional techniques; see response
Graham/SOMA	Structured and focused interviews, task and topic analysis, Kelly Grids, analysis of judgments
IE\O	CRC cards, importing components from libraries, elementary process discovery techniques (see response).
MTD	None
OBA	None
Objectory	None
OMT	Data dictionary, testing access paths, criteria for discarding associations and attributes
OOIE	Annotation of the models
SE/OT	None
SSADM4	No quick answer possible
Wirfs-Brock	Class and subsystem cards
Z++	None

D8 CHANGES TO THE TECHNICAL FRAMEWORK FOR OBJECT MODELING

Question

Does your method identify any other concepts which you think should be included in the object model? If yes, define the concepts (including how they are used).

Are there any model concepts which you think should be removed from the technical framework? If yes, give the name of the concept and the reason for its removal.

Findings

2 respondents said the definitions were not always clear. One said that the examples helped.

Most respondents told us of some additional concept that they would like to add, but there is no obvious commonality between them.

3 respondents seem to have a consensus opinion that several concepts are ill-defined, rather than superfluous.

OMT expressed doubt that the important differences between methodologies are well captured in any kind of uniform framework.

2 respondents recommended that concepts should be dropped from object modeling: Objectory advised us that Behavior, Quality, Deliverables, Schema, Architecture, and Techniques should all be removed.

Conclusions

We should determine whether there is any consensus over the additional concepts and, if there is, extend the technical framework.

But Objectory's opinion should also be considered. Perhaps it is inappropriate to include deliverables and activities in a section that describes a "common core" of object modeling principles that are applicable in all subject areas/life cycle stages.

Method	Technical framework, additions, deletions
Booch	None
CCM	Add account request event. More precise definitions.
C/Y/N	Add a multilayer concept. Add a multicomponent concept.
Demeter	Add propagation pattern.
Graham/SOMA	Add rule sets as distinct from assertions.
IE\O	Add occurrence (instance) and cover the properties of major object model concepts.
MTD	Add functional model as a specialized group and view concept.
OBA	None
Objectory	Give more precise definitions and relationships between terms (more than a simple hierarchy). Delete object behavior concepts, quality, deliverables, schema and architecture, techniques. These concepts are poorly defined or are irrelevant to object modeling.
OMT	Add meta-data, real-world objects, candidate key, generalization as extension and restriction, reasons for overriding operations. Deletions are no doubt necessary because any model is bound to have distortions.
OOIE	None
SE/OT	Add common event, reformulate constraint and assertion.
SSADM4	Add three schema architecture.
Wirfs-Brock	None
Z++	None

6

Strategic Modeling

INTRODUCTION

Strategic modeling seeks to provide a broad understanding of an enterprise and the domain in which it exists. It involves understanding the motivation behind, and planning to provide, a set of system solutions within that domain.

We asked the respondents the following questions:

- How is strategic modeling delineated in your method?
- What object structure concepts are used?
- Which rule concepts are used?
- Which group and view concepts do you use in strategic modeling?
- Which strategic modeling concepts are used?
- What are the deliverables of strategic modeling?
- Which activities do you use for strategic modeling?
- What techniques are used in strategic modeling?
- Are there any other features that should be included in strategic modeling, or any features that should be dropped?

Suppliers not covering strategic modeling were not required to answer this part of the survey. This part of the survey contains responses from 8 methods: C/Y/N, Graham/SOMA, IE\O, MTD, OBA, Objectory, OOIE, and Wirfs-Brock.

E1 PURPOSE

Question

E1.1 Does your method specifically delineate strategic modeling from the other areas of the technical framework?

Yes/No

E1.2 If it does, then explain how this is achieved.

Findings

5 methods claim comprehensive coverage of strategic modeling. These are:

- C/Y/N
- Graham/SOMA
- IE\O
- OOIE
- SSADM4

Of these 5, SSADM4 have not provided answers to the rest of the section. Graham/SOMA states that strategic modeling is not delineated from other areas of the technical framework, while the other three state that it is.

4 methods claim partial coverage of strategic modeling. These are:

- Booch
- MTD
- OBA
- Objectory

Of these 4, Booch has not provided answers to rest of the section. OBA and Objectory delineate strategic modeling from other areas of the technical framework, while MTD is less clear cut, and Booch does not delineate strategic modeling. Objectory's strategic modeling method is still under development.

While Wirfs-Brock does not claim to support strategic modeling, answers are provided to some of the questions.

6 respondents supplied comprehensive answers to the rest of section E:

- C/Y/N
- SOMA
- IE\O
- OBA
- Objectory
- OOIE

while MTD provided some answers.

Due to differences in the individual descriptions of strategic modeling, we suspect there is some divergence in what each of the suppliers see as the main focus of strategic modeling:

- Deciding what systems to develop in the future (what sequence, integration requirements, overall architectures, etc.) (IE\O and OOIE)
- Planning the adoption of object technology (in both the computer and end-user departments) (OBA?)
- Deciding radical ways to improve business processes through the use of information technology (Objectory, C/Y/N)
- Determining opportunities for reuse (OOIE, OBA)

Method	Delineated from other areas?	Answers? (1)	Coverage (2)
Booch	No	No	Partial
CCM	No	No	None
C/Y/N	Yes (9)	Yes	Comprehensive
Demeter	No	No	None
Graham/SOMA	No	Yes	Comprehensive
IE\O	Yes	Yes	Comprehensive
MTD	Qualified yes (3)	Partial	Partial
OBA	Yes (4)	Yes	Partial
Objectory	Yes (5)	Yes	Partial (under development)
OGROUP	No	No	None
OMT	No	No	None
OOIE	Yes (6)	Yes	Comprehensive
SE/OT	No, but (7)	No	None, but (7)
SSADM4	Yes (8)	No	Comprehensive
Wirfs-Brock	No	Partial	None
Z++	Not completed	No	None

Notes about the table

(1) This column indicates whether the respondent has answered questions E2–E8.
(2) This is the answer given to question A3.
(3) MTD currently treats organizational modeling aspects of strategic modeling as a lightweight form of analysis modeling.
(4) OBA itself provides some support for the concepts identified in "strategic modeling." However, it is the associated project management methodology—Prescription for Success (PFS)—that specifically delineates strategic modeling (reference given).
(5) Objectory explain the purpose of "business modeling"—which we must presume they equate with "strategic modeling." The purpose of "business modeling" is to develop a number of models that help us:

- describe and understand our business
- define major business goals
- understand where current practice should be changed to better reach the goals
- formulate input to the system development activities

(6) In OOIE, strategic modeling is a discrete stage of the method. It is not mandatory and is recommended where the aim is to build several cooperating systems and where reusability is a key goal. A strategic modeling project is distinguished by its aims, the level at which the modeling is carried out, and the emphasis on understanding motivation.

(7) Not included within the scope of SE/OT. Much strategic modeling is not specifically object-oriented. A separate method—LBMS Strategic Planning—addresses strategic modeling.

(8) Described in the SSADM4 subject guide "SSADM in an IS Strategy Environment." There was insufficient time to answer the rest of the strategic modeling section.

(9) C/Y/N. Called Object-Oriented Business Reengineering. Uses the same concepts, notation, and strategies that are used in OOA (analysis modeling).

Conclusions

Strategic modeling is not typically included in OO analysis and design methods.

This is, perhaps, not surprising, since object technology has had its main successes in the field of software engineering where any planning and analysis activities tend to be system-oriented rather than business-oriented. Information Systems development methods usually include—or have associated strategic planning—projects. Hence the "hybrid" methods, IE\O, OOIE, and SSADM4, all address this area.

E2   OBJECT STRUCTURE CONCEPTS

Question

The table below lists some object structure concepts identified in section 13.3.2 of the technical framework. You should read the section before answering this question.

E2.1 Please use the table to indicate whether you use the concept in strategic modeling (answer Yes/No column).

If you have renamed this concept in your method, please give your name in the alternative name column and provide your definition of this concept

Concept	Do you use it?	Alternative name or term
Strategic model concept	Yes/No	
Organization concept	Yes/No	
Real-world object type	Yes/No	

E2.2 Does your method use alternative definitions and/or other object structure concepts in strategic modeling?

Yes/No

E2.3   If yes, give a definition of these using the following template:

Concept _____

Definition _____

How it is used _____

Ref./Page _____

Findings

6 out of 8 methods use one or more organizational concepts. As shown in the table below, they use common terms such as "organizational unit." Wirfs-Brock can approximate to this concept.

4 respondents use real-world object types within strategic modeling.

Objectory state that they use 4 other strategic modeling concepts.

OOIE state that they use 6 other strategic modeling concepts. There is some overlap with the concepts IE\O chose to include under the heading "strategic modeling" (see their answer to question E5).

Method	Strategic model (1)	Organization	Real-world object type	Other OS concepts
C/Y/N	Yes	Yes	Yes, problem domain class	
Graham/SOMA	Yes	Yes	No	No
IE\O	N/a	Yes, org. unit, org. role, location	Yes, entity type	N/a
MTD	Yes	Yes, (2) org. unit, user type, work-group, user role	Yes	No
OBA	Yes	Yes	No	No
Objectory	No	No	No	Yes, (3) goal model, control model, interested external parties, business cases
OOIE	Yes, goal, mission, objective, CSF, customer satisfied, value stream	Yes, org. unit	Yes, business object	No
Wirfs-Brock	No	No, but (4)	No (5)	No

Notes about the table

(1) In the technical framework, Strategic Model Concept is the supertype of Organization Concept and Real-World Object Type. This question was redundant, since we offered the question "does your method support other object structure concepts in strategic modeling" in E2.

(2) MTD: definitions given in F2.3.

(3) Objectory: definitions provided.

(4) Wirfs-Brock: subsystems can approximate to this concept.

(5) Wirfs-Brock: no distinction is made between real-world and other object types.

Conclusions

There is fair agreement about the organizational concepts used in a strategic model but less agreement about the use of real-world object types as a special strategic model concept.

There is perhaps some confusion over whether these concepts should be classified as "strategic model" or "strategic modeling" concepts (see answers to question E5).

E3   RULE CONCEPTS

Question

Section 13.3.3 of the technical framework identifies one rule concept for strategic modeling. You should read the section before answering this question.

E3.1 Do you use the *business rule* in your method for strategic modeling?

Yes/No

E3.2 Does your method use an alternative definition and/or other rule concepts in strategic modeling?

Yes/No

E3.3 If yes, give a definition of these using the following template:

Rule _____

Definition _____

How it is used _____

Ref./Page _____

Findings

7 out of 8 methods employ business rules in strategic modeling, 3 of these methods (C/Y/N, Graham/SOMA, and IE\O) use exactly the same types of rules as they supply for object modeling.

The other rule concepts identified by Graham/SOMA and Objectory are already included in their responses to object modeling and strategic modeling respectively.

Method	Business rule used?	Other rule concepts?
C/Y/N	Yes	No
Graham/SOMA	Yes, as defined in object model	Yes, rule, rule set (1)
IE\O	Only those already defined in object model (4)	N/a
MTD	No	No
OBA	Yes	No
Objectory	Yes	Yes (2) goal model, control model
OOIE	Yes	No, see object model (3)
Wirfs-Brock	Indeterminate	

Notes about the table

(1) Graham/SOMA: these concepts are those already defined in the object model section D3.3.
(2) Objectory: these concepts were also offered as strategic modeling "object structure concepts" in answer to E2, where they are defined.
(3) OOIE's object model (in D3.3) includes 16 rule types, although these are not individually defined in their response.
(4) IE\O's object model (in D3.3) names seven types of rule.

Conclusions

Business rules are widely supported by the methods which address strategic modeling. The survey does not clearly identify the nature of these rules.

E4   GROUP AND VIEW CONCEPTS

Question

The table below lists some group and view concepts identified in section 13.3.4 of the technical framework. You should read the section before answering this question.

E4.1 Please use the table to indicate whether you use the concept in your strategic modeling (answer Yes/No column).

If you have renamed this concept in your method, please give your name in the alternative name column and provide your definition of this concept.

Concept	Do you use it?	Alternative name or term
Business process model	Yes/No	
Architecture concept	Yes/No	

E4.2 Does your method use alternative definitions and/or other group and view concepts in strategic modeling?

> Yes/No

E4.3 If yes, give a definition of these using the following template:

> Concept _____
>
> Definition _____
>
> How it is used _____
>
> Ref./Page _____

Findings

6 out of 8 of the methods employ a business process model concept.

4 out of 8 methods employ architecture concepts: IE\O and OOIE specify a number of different architectures which appear to have some similarity.

4 out of 8 methods identify other group and view concepts. 14 different concepts get mentioned with no commonality between them.

Method	Business process model?	Architecture concept?	Other G+V concept?
C/Y/N	Yes	No	No
Graham/SOMA	Yes	No	No
IE\O	Yes, uses: business function, process, dependency, etc.	Yes (1), information architecture, systems architecture, technical architecture, information management architecture	Yes (1), system development plan, business strategy assessment, business area, (proposed) system, reusable component, subject area, activity cluster, data cluster
MTD	Yes	No	Yes, organization, structure model (2)
OBA	No	No	No
Objectory	Yes	Yes	Yes (3), ideal business object model, resource model
OOIE	Yes	Yes (4), business object architecture, presentation object architecture, implementation object architecture, technical architecture, organization architecture	Yes(4), object relationship diagram, object flow diagram, event diagram
Wirfs-Brock	No	Yes, subsystem	No

Notes about the table

(1) IE\O: no definitions given, only a reference.

(2) MTD: the Organization structure model is in terms of organizational units and the user types and the user roles they support; this model is effectively a specification of a whole-part model.

(3) Objectory definitions:
- Ideal business object model: it includes the business cases, but not the organizational part. It is used as input to the continuous refinement of the business, including the development of computer-based support.
- Resource model: the major resources needed in the business. Used as guidance to the rest of the modeling.

(4) OOIE: no definitions given.

Conclusions

There is fair agreement that business process models should be built and some agreement over architectural concepts but the diversity of "other concepts" indicates that this is an area where different methods have unique capabilities.

E5 MODELING CONCEPTS

Question

The table below lists some modeling concepts identified in section 13.3.5 of the technical framework. You should read the section before answering this question.

E5.1 Please use the table to indicate whether you use the concept in strategic modeling (answer Yes/No column).

If you have renamed this concept in your method, please give your name in the alternative name column and provide your definition of this concept.

Concept	Do you use it?	Alternative name or term
Strategic modeling	Yes/No	
Enterprise concept	Yes/No	
Motivation concept	Yes/No	

E5.2 Does your method use alternative definitions and/or other modeling concepts in strategic modeling?

Yes/No

E5.3 If yes, give a definition of these using the following template:

Concept _____

Definition _____

How it is used _____

Ref./Page _____

Findings

7 out of 8 methods employ enterprise concepts; only 2 methods elaborate on the concepts they support (the technical framework gives examples of 8 concepts).

7 out of 8 methods support motivation concepts; the technical framework gives examples of 7 of these.

3 out of 8 methods support other strategic modeling concepts; 13 further concepts are listed, although IE\O do not make it clear which ones were enterprise and which were motivational concepts. C/Y/N chose to include business process reengineering as a strategic modeling concept.

Method	Enterprise concept?	Motivation concept?	Other SM concept? (1)
C/Y/N	Yes	Yes	Yes (5)
Graham/SOMA	Yes	Yes	No
IE\O	Yes, see other SM concepts	Yes, see other SM concepts	Yes (2), critical success factor, goal, mission, information need, information need category, objective, strategy, performance measure, current (information) system, current data store
MTD	Yes	Yes	No
OBA	Yes	Yes	No
Objectory (3)	Yes, (business concept)	Yes	Yes (4), control modeling, goal modeling
OOIE	Yes	Yes	No
Wirfs-Brock	Indeterminate		

Notes about the table

(1) Answers to the first concept in E5.1 (Strategic modeling—Do you use it?) have been ignored, since the question is superfluous and possibly misleading. "Strategic modeling" should have read "Strategic Modeling Concept," so it may have been misinterpreted. It is the supertype of the next two concepts we ask about, and we go on to ask if there any other concepts under the strategic modeling heading (in question E5.2).
(2) IE\O: no definitions given, although a reference is.
(3) Objectory use the term "Business Modeling" in preference to "Strategic Modeling."
(4) Objectory: these concepts are defined in E2. (They are also included in the response to Object Structure Concepts, Rule Concepts, and [here] Strategic Model concepts.)
(5) C/Y/N: Object-Oriented Business Reengineering (OOBRM). There are three filtered kinds of views in the model: the as-is view, the business view, and the alternative views.

Conclusion

There is confusion over whether these concepts should be included under strategic modeling concepts or under strategic model concepts (see question E2). For example IE\O and OOIE have listed 4 concepts (e.g., goal, mission, objective, and critical success factor) which they have in common under these different headings.

E6   DELIVERABLES

Question

Does your method describe major deliverables resulting from strategic modeling?
The table below lists some deliverables identified in section 13.4 of the technical framework. You should read the section before answering this question.

E6.1   Please use the table to indicate whether your method provides the deliverable during strategic modeling:

Deliverable	Do you use it?
Mission statement	Yes/No
Models	Yes/No
Recommendations	Yes/No
Issues	Yes/No
System boundary definitions	Yes/No
System architectures	Yes/No
Resource statement	Yes/No
Development plans	Yes/No

E6.2   Does your method describe any other deliverables from strategic modeling?
Yes/No

E6.3   If yes, give a description of these using the following template:
Deliverable _____
Description _____
Use _____
Ref./Page _____

Findings

The findings have been separated into three parts with a set of conclusions at the end.

Useful responses were received from 7 of the submitters.

Part 1: Mission statement, models, and recommendations

4 out of 7 methods include mission statements or statements of direction. One of these states the mission statement is optional; another states it is "input."

5 out of 7 methods include models of object types with their relationships and behaviors.

6 out of 7 methods include recommendations within strategic modeling.

Method	Mission statement?	Models?	Recommendations?
C/Y/N	Yes	Yes	Yes
Graham/SOMA	Yes, optional	Yes	Yes
IE\O	No, it's input	Yes, Information Model	Yes, 4 architectures, a development plan, and supporting text
MTD	N/a	N/a	Yes
OBA	Yes	No	Yes
Objectory (3)	No	Yes	No
OOIE	Yes	Yes	Yes
Wirfs-Brock (1)	N/a	N/a	N/a

Part 2: Issues, system boundary definitions, and system architectures

5 out of 7 methods cover issues. One other method stated it is "likely" that the user of the method will identify issues.

6 out of 7 methods include systems boundary definitions to scope the system. One of these 6 includes boundary definitions within another deliverable.

5 out of 7 methods include a systems architecture. One of these 5 includes systems architecture information within another deliverable.

Method	Issues?	System boundary definitions?	System architectures?
C/Y/N	Yes	Yes (1)	Yes (1)
Graham/SOMA	Yes, optional	Yes	No
IE\O	Not mandatory, but likely	Yes, within system definitions of the systems architecture	Yes
MTD	Yes	N/a	N/a
OBA	Yes	Yes	Yes, indirectly through system development goals and objectives

Method	Issues?	System boundary definitions?	System architectures?
Objectory	No	Yes	Yes
OOIE	Yes	Yes	Yes
Wirfs-Brock (1)	N/a	N/a	N/a

Notes about the table

(1) C/Y/N. Yes—in the sense of understanding the system in a much broader context than just an automated system.

Part 3: Resource statements, development plans, and other deliverables

4 out of 7 methods include resource statements. One of these methods includes this information within another deliverable.

4 out of 7 methods include development plans. One other method states that development plans are "optional."

There are 10 other deliverables listed which appear to have little commonality.

Method	Resource statement?	Development plans?	Other deliverables?
C/Y/N	Yes (4)	Yes (5)	No
Graham/SOMA	No	No (optional)	Software simulation of business (optional)
IE\O	Yes (within development plan)	Yes	Business strategy assessment
MTD	N/a	N/a	Strategies for IT development
OBA	Yes	Yes	Training plan, Reuse plan, Measurement plan (2)
Objectory	No (3)	No	Business case descriptions, Business object description
OOIE	Yes	Yes	Objectives, Critical success factors
Wirfs-Brock (1)	N/a	N/a	N/a

Notes about the table

(1) Wirfs-Brock: a complete design consists of hierarchy graphs and collaboration graphs for all of the classes in the application or framework. Specifications for each class, subsystem, and contract are also part of the design.

(2) OBA deliverables include:
- Training plan: a statement of how to get the employees of the organization up to speed in the use of OO technology. Typically covers some or all subsequent projects, not just the first project.
- Reuse plan: a description of how the organization will structure itself for effective long-term reuse. Used to establish new teams (if necessary) as well as the organization's policies regarding the 12 reuse activities (see reference).
- Measurement plan: describes the various process, product, and resource measures that are to be collected during all projects within the organization. Used to correct problems in ongoing projects or to establish new procedures to avoid problems in future projects.

(3) Objectory deliverables include:
- Business case descriptions: which describe the *cases* in the business and are used as input to enhance the enterprise.
- Business object descriptions: which describe the *processes* in the business and are used as input to enhance the enterprise.

(4) C/Y/N: Yes, in the sense of understanding the "resource" in a much broader context than just computational resources.

(5) C/Y/N: Yes—only a very high level of planning.

Conclusions

The overall conclusion is that the technical framework provides a reasonable coverage of strategic modeling deliverables. But the survey responses identified 10 other deliverables which could be used to extend the scope and coverage of the framework.

E7   ACTIVITIES

Question

The table below lists some activities identified in section 13.5 of the technical framework for strategic modeling. You should read the section before answering this question.

E7.1 Please use the table to indicate whether you use the activity in strategic modeling (answer Yes/No column).

If you have renamed this activity in your method, please give your name in the alternative name column and provide your definition of this activity.

Activity	Do you use it?	Alternative name or term
Plan	Yes/No	
Outline	Yes/No	
Understand	Yes/No	
Architect	Yes/No	

E7.2   Does your method use alternative definitions and/or other activities to produce deliverables in strategic modeling?

Yes/No

E7.3   If yes, give a definition of these using the following template:

Activity _____

Definition _____

How it is used _____

Ref./Page _____

Findings

There were 6 responses to this question which could be used as a basis for these findings.

5 methods include a "plan" activity.

3 methods include an "outline" activity.

4 methods include an "understand" activity.

3 methods include an "architect" activity.

3 methods have identified "other" activities:

- OOIE identified a "finalize plan" activity
- Objectory placed all 4 of their strategic modeling activities in the "other" category.

1 method had a perfect fit with the technical framework.

1 method had an entirely different view of the activity types involved in strategic modeling.

The 3 other methods had a partial correspondence.

The technical framework also included a "decide" activity, but this was missing from the questionnaire and has not been included in these findings.

Method	Plan?	Outline?	Understand?	Architect?	Other?
C/Y/N	Yes	Yes	Yes	Yes	Yes
Graham/SOMA	Yes	No	Yes	No	No
IE\O	Yes, in: Plan the ISP stage	No	Yes, in: Make initial assessment, Assess the current environment	Yes, in: Define the information architecture, Define the systems architecture, Define the technical architecture	No (1)

Method	Plan?	Outline?	Understand?	Architect?	Other?
MTD	N/a	N/a	N/a	N/a	N/a
OBA	Yes	Yes	No	No	No
Objectory	No	No	No	No	Yes, in (2): Identify business, Delimit business, Analyze business, Design business
OOIE	Yes	Yes	Yes	Yes	Yes: Finalize Plan (3)
Wirfs-Brock	Indeterminate, none apparent				

Notes about the table

(1) IE\O: all activities are covered within the 7 major activities given already.

(2) Objectory: the additional activities are defined as follows:
  - Identify business: identifies the business goals, control mechanisms, and supporting resources; used as a base for business modeling.
  - Delimit business: identifies the business cases of the business in focus; used as a base for planning business enhancement.
  - Analyze business: identifies the participating business objects needed to support the business dynamics; used as a base for defining the actual processes needed.
  - Design business: describes the real business objects needed in the business; used as a definition of a business model.

(3) OOIE. The "finalize plan" activity is the last activity of the strategic modeling stage. It turns the architectures into a practical plan for implementation.

(4) C/Y/N. Five additional activities were named and defined.
  - Modeling the business: people, organizations, and forms.
    — Develops the OOBR model/as-is view: it models the people, organizations, and forms (screens, data entry forms, and printed reports) currently used by the business enterprise.
    — Involves building a class and object model of the business enterprise; classes will correspond to people, the roles people play, organizations, and forms.
  - Modeling the business: crossing the boundaries.
    — Develops the OOBR model/business view—a class-and-object model free of the people, organizational, or forms of physical packaging of knowledge and responsibilities.
    — Involves building a view of the initial people/organizations/form model. Removes duplicate knowledge and responsibility. Identifies problem domain classes and objects. Moves knowledge and responsibilities into corresponding class symbols.

- Modeling the business: acting out scenarios.
  - Develops the object interactions to the OOBR model/business view.
  - Involves acting out the dynamics. Refines allocation of knowledge and responsibilities. Delegates as much work as possible to individuals; lets managers coordinate across a collection of team members.
- Modeling the business: adding rules and conventions.
  - Adds rules and constraints to the OOBR model/business view.
  - Involves adding the rules and constraints that apply to each business domain class and the objects in that class.
- Modeling the business: defining new processes.
  - Results in the OOBR model/alternative views—ones that propose a different way to organize object knowledge, responsibilities, and interactions—to achieve goals within constraints.
  - Involves adding containers to represent what each person, organization, or form knows and does; acting out corresponding interactions; trying out alternatives, based on critical success factors (e.g., minimize staff count, minimize total salary amount, minimize waiting time for customer, minimize errors).

Conclusions

Methods support a variety of activity types and it is questionable whether it is useful to include activity types in a technical framework.

E8   TECHNIQUES

Question

E8.1   Which of the techniques identified in section 13.6 of the technical framework do you employ during strategic modeling?

E8.2   Does your method use any other techniques during strategic modeling?
Yes/No

E8.3   If yes, give a definition of these using the following template:
Technique _____
Definition _____
How it is used _____
Ref./Page _____

Findings

The number of methods that employ each technique listed in the technical framework is given below.

Exploitable answers were received for 5 methods. OBA answered "most of them," so we decided to disregard their response in the list below.

Technique	No. of methods using it
Meetings	4
Project planning	2
Interviewing	5
Consolidation of ideas and implications	3
Strategic object modeling	5
Matrix modeling	3
Generic modeling	1
Presentation	2
Quality assurance	1
Feasibility study	1
System sizing	1
Scheduling	1
Resource estimation	2
Data flow diagramming	0
Function dependency diagramming	2
Use of visual aids	2
Report writing	2
Tasks and deliverables	1
Feedback	2
SWOT (= strengths, weaknesses, opportunities, threats)	1
Consensus seeking	2

IE\O identified 9 further techniques which they employ.

Method	Technical framework techniques used	Other techniques used
C/Y/N	Meetings, interviewing, consolidation of ideas and implications, strategic object modeling	No
Graham/SOMA	Interviewing, strategic object modeling, matrix modeling, presentation, feasibility study, feedback, SWOT, consensus seeking	No

Method	Technical framework techniques used	Other techniques used
IE\O	Meetings, project planning, interviewing, strategic object modeling, matrix modeling, function dependency diagramming, resource estimation, use of visual aids, report writing	Yes, Executive intensive planning workshops, Functional decomposition, Reusable component identification, Current systems analysis, Business process reengineering, Cluster analysis, RAEW analysis, System prioritization techniques, Cost-benefit analysis
MTD	N/a	N/a
OBA	Most of them	Anything else that is appropriate
Objectory	Meetings, interviewing, consolidation, strategic object modeling (2)	Yes (1)
OOIE	All listed techniques except: feasibility study, data flow diagramming, SWOT	No
Wirfs-Brock	Indeterminate, none apparent	

Notes about the table

(1) Objectory: state that "other techniques" are used in strategic modeling, but do not explain what they are, except to say "see above." Do they mean goal and control modeling?

(2) Objectory: emphasize that strategic object modeling is *the* technique of strategic modeling!

Conclusions

The small number of responses make it difficult to draw useful conclusions, except to say there is no real strong consensus on strategic modeling techniques.

Interviewing and meetings are the only widely employed techniques; it would be difficult to imagine that strategic modeling did not involve some kind of strategic modeling technique, or is performed without meetings or interviews.

More detailed research in this area will interest methodologists, system architects, and enterprise planners, but is probably of marginal interest to the object technologists.

E9 CHANGES TO THE TECHNICAL FRAMEWORK FOR STRATEGIC MODELING

Question

E9.1 Does your method identify any other feature which you think should be included in the strategic model?

E9.2   Are there features in analysis modeling which you think should be removed from the strategic model?

Yes/No

E9.3   If yes, specify the feature and give your reason for its removal:

Feature _____

Reason for removal _____

Findings

2 respondents stated that further features should be included within strategic modeling.

- Objectory advise that "enterprise dynamics" should be included in strategic modeling, since the technical framework gives only static view of the business.
- C/Y/N recommends the use of multilayer and multicomponent concepts.

Method	Further features?	Features to be dropped? (3)
C/Y/N	Multilayer concept (2), multicomponent concept (3)	
Graham/SOMA	N/a	No
IE\O	N/a	N/a
MTD	N/a	N/a
OBA	No	No
Objectory	Yes, enterprise dynamics (1)	Yes (5)
OOIE	N/a	No
Wirfs-Brock	Indeterminate	

Notes about the table

(1) Question E9.2 asks if any analysis modeling features should be removed from the strategic model. This question may have been answered literally, or interpreted by the respondent.
(2) C/Y/N: recommends adding a multilayer concept. A modeling notation that allows the selection of the level of detail to be displayed—spanning classes, objects, attributes, connections, services, and messages. (Provided under response to question D8—but reiterated in the strategic modeling response.)
(3) C/Y/N: recommends adding a multicomponent concept. A modeling notation that supports loose coupling between the major categories of classes in a design, e.g., problem domain classes, human interaction classes, task management classes, and data management classes. (Provided under response to question D8—but reiterated in the strategic modeling response.)

(4) Objectory: the most important task during business modeling (i.e., strategic modeling) is to capture the dynamics of the enterprise, what we call cases. There is nothing about this in the technical framework.

(5) Objectory: there seems to be an underlying assumption that we model a static, existing view of a business. This assumption is unfortunate and gives a too-static view of the business as it is currently organized.

Conclusion

Extend the technical framework to address dynamics within strategic modeling.

The multilayer concept is a useful presentation/diagramming technique, but does not impact the technical framework and need not be confined to strategic modeling.

The use of multiple loosely coupled object models is not confined to strategic modeling and is not ruled out by the technical framework, which recognizes various categories of object type in other areas (e.g., user interface object type, data management object type, problem domain object type). Perhaps "model" should be represented in the technical framework under Group-and-view concept.

7

Analysis Modeling

INTRODUCTION

Analysis modeling obtains a thorough description of a problem domain. The survey asked questions about the following:

- How is analysis modeling delineated from other areas in your method?
- What object structure concepts are used?
- Which rule concepts are used?
- Which group and view concepts are used?
- Which analysis modeling concepts are used?
- What are the deliverables of analysis modeling ?
- Which activities are used?
- What techniques are used in analysis modeling?
- Are there any other features that should be included in analysis modeling, or any features that should be dropped?

One method (OGROUP) does not address analysis modeling, therefore the survey responses for this method are missing. The following findings and conclusions apply to the remaining 15 methods.

Note: Booch answered only question F4: Group and view concepts.

F1   PURPOSE

Questions

F1.1 Does your method specifically delineate analysis modeling from the other areas of the technical framework?

     Yes/No

F1.2 If it does, explain how this is achieved.

Findings

14 methods answered this question.

4 methods, CCM, Demeter, Graham/SOMA, Wirfs-Brock, do not delineate analysis modeling from the other areas.

The majority of responses, 10 out of 15, differentiate analysis from the other areas.

8 methods, C/Y/N, IE\O, OBA, Objectory, OOIE, OMT, SE/OT, Z++, delineate analysis by focusing on the problem domain objects while not addressing design issues.

Conclusions

Most methods delineate analysis from other areas.

    Different methods use different approaches to delineate analysis from other areas. Some methods use a set of concepts throughout the life cycle, which is extended as development proceeds from analysis to design to implementation. Others use different sets of concepts for different areas.

Method	Comments
Booch	No response
CCM	No
C/Y/N	Yes, OOA works with problem domain classes; OOD delineates design modeling by working with human interaction, task management, and data management classes
Demeter	No
Graham/SOMA	No
IE\O	Yes, analysis modeling is free from design issues
MTD	Yes, by teaching the relevant parts of object modeling
OBA	Yes, by focusing on aspects of problem model
Objectory	Yes, separate process called "requirements analysis"

Method	Comments
OMT	Yes, by capturing real-world perspective, external view of system, requirements, concentrates on *what*
OOIE	Yes, by focusing on the description of business or problem domain using business objects
SE/OT	Yes, by capturing real-world objects in problem domain, kept distinct from the application model
SSADM4	Yes, stages 1,2,3: analysis of the OMG technical framework maps to SSADM4 conceptual model
Wirfs-Brock	No
Z++	Yes, analysis model corresponds to domain analysis and requirements capture

F2   OBJECT STRUCTURE CONCEPTS

Question

The table below lists some object structure concepts identified in section 14.3.2 of the technical framework. You should read the section before answering this question.

F2.1 Please use the table to indicate whether you use the concept in analysis modeling (answer Yes/No column).

If you have renamed this concept in your method, please give your name in the alternative name column and provide your definition of this concept.

Concept	Do you use it?	Alternative name or term
Problem domain object type	Yes/No	
Abstract object type	Yes/No	
Functional concept	Yes/No	

F2.2 Does your method use alternative definitions and/or other object structure concepts in analysis modeling?
Yes/No

F2.3 If yes, give a definition of these using the following template:
Concept _____
Definition _____
How it is used _____
Ref./Page _____

Findings

This section effectively asks four questions; each of the sections which follow contain the replies to one of these questions.

Problem domain object type

14 methods use the concept of problem domain object types.

3 methods, MTD, OBA, Z++, use the term "problem domain object type."

5 methods, CCM, C/Y/N, Demeter, SOMA, Wirfs-Brock, use the alternative term "class."

Method	Comments
Booch	No response
CCM	Yes, alternative name: class
C/Y/N	Yes, problem domain class
Demeter	Yes, alternative name: class
Graham/SOMA	Yes, alternative name: class
IE\O	Yes, alternative name: entity type
MTD	Yes
OBA	Yes
Objectory	Yes, alternative name: domain object
OMT	Yes, but not differentiated from objects used in object modeling
OOIE	Yes, alternative name: business object type
SE/OT	Yes, alternative name: shared object type
SSADM4	Yes, alternative name: entity
Wirfs-Brock	Yes, alternative name: class; no distinction between problem domain and other object types
Z++	Yes

Abstract object type

13 methods use this concept.

4 methods, CCM, C/Y/N, Demeter, and Graham/SOMA, use the alternative name "class."

3 use the same alternative name as for problem domain object type.

Objectory does not use the concept.

CCM questions the value of the distinction between real-world object types and abstract object types.

Method	Comments
Booch	No response
CCM	Yes, alternative name: class
C/Y/N	Yes, alternative name: class
Demeter	Yes, alternative name: alternation class
Graham/SOMA	Yes, alternative name: class
IE\O	Yes, alternative name: abstract entity type
MTD	Yes
OBA	Yes
Objectory	No
OMT	Yes, but not special to analysis modeling
OOIE	Yes
SE/OT	Yes
SSADM4	Yes, alternative name: entity, LDM entry point
Wirfs-Brock	Yes, alternative name: abstract class
Z++	Yes

Functional concept

10 methods use this concept; only 3 use exactly that term.

Alternative names include: "class," "function," "process," "script," "use case," "event," "inquiry," and "operation."

CCM suggests that the definition in the technical framework is so vague as to be unusable.

Method	Comments
Booch	No response
CCM	CCM supports operations, but not functional concepts that would span classes
C/Y/N	No
Demeter	Yes
Graham/SOMA	Yes, alternative name: class, layer, implemented-by link
IE\O	Yes, alternative names: (business) function, process, elementary process
MTD	Yes
OBA	Yes, alternative name: script
Objectory	Yes, alternative name: use case

Method	Comments
OMT	Yes, alternative names: process (as in DFD's, function; appears to be a synonym for process), activity and action (appear in SRD's, part of the dynamic model)
OOIE	Yes, alternative name: operation
SE/OT	No
SSADM4	Yes, alternative names: event, inquiry
Wirfs-Brock	No
Z++	Yes

Additional object structure concepts and definitions for these concepts

Some respondents put concepts here which they noted as alternative names for other object structure concepts. Examples are: "script" by OBA, and "use case" and "domain object" by Objectory.

Additional concepts identified are: generic user, work group, user role, task, actor, process type, real-world object type, and domain object.

Real-world object type and domain object have also been suggested as additional concepts, although problem domain object type is in the technical framework. The same applies for associations.

Method	Comments
Booch	No response
CCM	No
C/Y/N	Yes, Class as defined in *Webster's New Twentieth Century Dictionary*: A class is a number of people or things grouped because of certain likenesses or common traits
Demeter	Yes, no further description
Graham/SOMA	No
IE\O	Yes, functional concepts (see preceding table)
MTD	Yes, generic user, work group, user role, task, process type, real-world object type
OBA	Yes, alternative names: scripting, party role classification
Objectory	Yes, use case, domain object, actor
OMT	No response
OOIE	No
SE/OT	No
SSADM4	Yes
Wirfs-Brock	Yes, as described in object modeling
Z++	Yes, associations which are relationships between object types

Conclusions

Most methods include the concept of problem domain object type, but use alternative names for the concept.

Most methods include the concept of an abstract object type.

Most methods include the concept of a function concept but use alternative names for the concept.

Some of the additional object structure concepts listed by the respondents are similar to previously identified concepts or seem to be alternative names for them. Therefore the distinctive nature of these additional concepts is not clear.

F3   RULE CONCEPT

Question

Section 14.3.3 of the technical framework identifies one rule concept. You should read the section before answering this question.

F3.1   Does your method use rule concepts in analysis modeling?
Yes/No

F3.2   If yes, give a definition of these using the following template:
Concept _____
Definition _____
How it is used _____
Ref./Page _____

Findings

12 methods use the concept of rules.

7 of them refer to their concept of rules used in their object modeling section.

2 methods, Objectory and Wirfs-Brock, do not use this concept.

Graham/SOMA regards rules as very important; rules as part of an object discriminate its methods.

Conclusions

Most of the methods surveyed include a rules concept.

The survey shows that the concept used in analysis modeling should be a reuse of the rules concept used in object modeling.

Method	Comments
Booch	No response
CCM	Yes, as in object modeling
C/Y/N	Yes, as in object modeling
Demeter	Yes
Graham/SOMA	Yes, rule set as in object modeling (see answer to question D3), used to encode business rules, high-order constraints and assertions for discussions with users and domain experts. Also used to specify global control structures and regimes
IE\O	Yes, as in object modeling
MTD	Yes, constraint to model real-world constraints on any solution created to satisfy this problem domain
OBA	Yes, "goals" and "objectives," "precondition/postcondition," "sequencing constraint"
Objectory	No
OMT	Yes, as in object modeling
OOIE	Yes, as in object modeling
SE/OT	Yes, object type invariant constraints on attributes and relationships of objects that have to be true at all times, "general static constraint," any multi-object constraint
SSADM4	Yes, as in object modeling
Wirfs-Brock	No
Z++	Yes, "constraints," semantic constraints, expressed in natural language or mathematics, on object or process models, used to express domain knowledge, which cannot be expressed in the syntax of the diagrams

F4   ANALYSIS MODEL GROUP AND VIEW CONCEPTS

Question

The table on page 95 lists some concepts identified in section 14.3.4 of the technical framework. You should read the section before answering this question.

F4.1   Please use the table to indicate whether you use the concept in analysis modeling (answer Yes/No column).

If you have renamed this concept in your method, please give your name in the alternative name column and provide your definition of this concept.

Concept	Do you use it?	Alternative name or term
Structural model	Yes/No	
Subject area	Yes/No	
Behavioral model	Yes/No	
Functional model	Yes/No	
Application	Yes/No	
Quality Goals	Yes/No	

F4.2 Does your method use alternative definitions and/or other group and view concepts in analysis modeling?

Yes/No

F4.3 If yes, give a definition of these using the following template:

Concept _____

Definition _____

How it is used _____

Ref./Page _____

Findings

This section effectively asks seven questions; each of the sections which follow addresses the replies to one of these questions.

Structural model

14 methods use this concept. Wirfs-Brock answered no, but uses similar concepts which are hierarchy and collaboration graphs.

4 methods, C/Y/N, Graham/SOMA, OMT, Z++, use the alternative term "object model."

IE\O uses two alternative names/concepts.

Method	Comments
Booch	Yes
CCM	Yes, alternative name: part of "class" and "information diagram." If the technical framework was defined with a dual life cycle model (e.g., class analysis and design versus application analysis), structural models are detail views, not group views, in class analysis
C/Y/N	Yes, class and object model
Demeter	Yes, alternative name: "class dictionary graph"
Graham/SOMA	Yes, alternative name: "object model"

Method	Comments
IE\O	Yes, alternative names: "entity life cycle diagrams" and "entity model" depicted in "em diagram," "em list," "em browser," "collaboration diagram"
MTD	Yes
OBA	Yes, alternative name: "static model"
Objectory	Yes, alternative name: "various views"
OMT	Yes, alternative name: "object model"
OOIE	Yes, alternative names: "object relationship diagram," "structural rules"
SE/OT	Yes, alternative name: "static view"
SSADM4	Yes, alternative name: "logical data model"
Wirfs-Brock	No, but similar to hierarchy and collaboration graphs
Z++	Yes, alternative name: "object model"

Subject area

12 methods use this concept; 5 use exactly this term.

CCM does not use it because this is part of their "network view."

Wirfs-Brock does not use this concept, but mentions a similar concept, called "subsystems."

Method	Comments
Booch	Yes
CCM	No, because this more the "network view," CCM supports the "node view"
C/Y/N	Yes, alternative names: class and object model
Demeter	Yes, alternative names: "component," "partial class dictionary graph"
Graham/SOMA	Yes, alternative name: "layer"
IE\O	Yes
MTD	Yes
OBA	Yes
Objectory	Yes, alternative name: "package"
OMT	Yes, alternative names: "module," "sheet"
OOIE	Yes
SE/OT	Yes, alternative name: "object model subset"
SSADM4	Yes, alternative name: "partitioned logical data model"
Wirfs-Brock	No, but approximation by "subsystems"
Z++	No

Behavioral model

13 methods use the concept.

CCM answers yes, but does not particularly name the concept; it is part of several diagrams.

IE\O mentions 2 alternative names/concepts depicted in various forms.

Only 2 methods, Booch and Demeter, use the term "behavioral model"; 3 methods use the alternate name "dynamic model."

Method	Comments
Booch	Yes
CCM	Yes, not explicitly named, but shown in several diagrams. If the technical framework was defined with a dual life cycle model (e.g., class analysis and design versus application analysis), behavioral models are detail views, not group views, in class analysis
C/Y/N	Yes, alternative names: "class and object model"
Demeter	Yes
Graham/SOMA	Yes, alternative name: "dynamics model"
IE\O	Yes, alternative names: "event or control model" depicted in "event list," "event response diagram," "state transition diagrams"; "behavior definition," defined in "operation request diagrams," "method hierarchies," "method action diagrams," "method rule diagram"
MTD	No
OBA	Yes, alternative name: "dynamic model"
Objectory	Yes, alternative name: "use case"
OMT	Yes, alternative names: "dynamic model"
OOIE	Yes, alternative names: "event diagram" "behavioral rules"
SE/OT	Yes, alternative name: "dynamic view"
SSADM4	Yes, alternative name: "entity event model"
Wirfs-Brock	No, behavior is restricted to responsibilities, methods, messages and signatures
Z++	Yes, alternative name: "state chart"

Functional model

6 methods use this concept, 3 with this term; 9 methods do not use this concept.

Again, IE\O uses five diagram types for this model.

Data flow diagram is used 3 times (OMT does not name it in the survey, but in his method description).

Method	Comments
Booch	No
CCM	No, not as defined in the technical framework
C/Y/N	No
Demeter	No
Graham/SOMA	No
IE\O	Yes, depicted in "process hierarchy diagram," "process dependency diagram," "data flow diagram," "process/entity type matrix" (= "business operation/object type matrix")
MTD	Yes
OBA	No
Objectory	No
OMT	Yes
OOIE	Yes
SE/OT	No
SSADM4	Yes, alternative names: "effect correspondence diagram," "inquiry access path"
Wirfs-Brock	No
Z++	Yes, alternative name: "data flow diagram"

Application

9 methods use the concept, 6 do not.

Alternative names are "system scoping," "update and enquiry process model."

Method	Comments
Booch	No
CCM	No, but "classes" modeled are intended to be reused in applications
C/Y/N	Yes, alternative names: class and object model
Demeter	Yes
Graham/SOMA	No
IE\O	Yes, the operations to be supported by each system are depicted in "system scoping diagram"
MTD	Yes
OBA	Yes
Objectory	Yes

Method	Comments
OMT	No
OOIE	Yes
SE/OT	No
SSADM4	Yes, alternative name: "update and enquiry process model"
Wirfs-Brock	Yes
Z++	No

Quality goals

9 methods use this concept, 6 do not.

Method	Comments
Booch	No
CCM	No
C/Y/N	Yes, class and object model
Demeter	Yes
Graham/SOMA	Yes, alternative names: "class descriptions," "service levels," "volumetrics"
IE\O	Yes, alternative name: "system acceptance criteria"
MTD	Yes
OBA	Yes
Objectory	No
OMT	No
OOIE	Yes
SE/OT	Yes, alternative name: "nonfunctional attributes"
SSADM4	Yes
Wirfs-Brock	No
Z++	No

Alternative or other group and view concepts with definitions

7 methods answered no.

SSADM4 answered "no quick answer possible."

The OMT response suggested that "model" be included as a concept within the technical framework. A model is a distinct concept from a diagram of that model.

Method	Comments
Booch	No response
CCM	No response
C/Y/N	Yes, see reply to question D4.5
Demeter	Yes
Graham/SOMA	No
IE\O	No
MTD	Yes, "task model," "process model," "user-role model," "usability goals"
OBA	No
Objectory	No
OMT	Yes, various diagrams describe aspects of behavioral and functional models: "state diagram," "event flow diagram," "event trace diagram," "scenario," "data flow diagram"
OOIE	No
SE/OT	No
SSADM4	No quick answer possible
Wirfs-Brock	Yes, refers to object modeling
Z++	No

Conclusions

Most of the methods include the concept of a structural model, but most methods use an alternative name for the concept.

Most of the methods include a concept of a subject area.

Most of the methods include the concept of a behavioral model.

The functional model concept is not supported by many methods; there may be a case for removing it from the technical framework.

The application and quality goal concepts are not overwhelmingly supported.

Most of the methods do not have alternative definitions of the group and view concepts in analysis modeling.

F5   MODELING CONCEPT

Question

The table on page 101 lists some concepts identified in section 14.3.5 of the technical framework. You should read the section before answering this question.

F5.1 Please use the table to indicate whether you use the concept in analysis modeling (answer Yes/No column).

If you have renamed this concept in your method, please give your name in the alternative name column and provide your definition of this concept.

Concept	Do you use it?	Alternative name or term
Human factors	Yes/No	
Marketing	Yes/No	
Problem statement	Yes/No	
Development priority	Yes/No	

F5.2 Does your method use alternative definitions and/or other modeling concepts in analysis modeling?

Yes/No

F5.3 If yes, give a definition of these using the following template:

Concept _____

Definition _____

How it is used _____

Ref./Page _____

Findings

Human factors concept

9 methods answered yes, 2 answered no.

Alternative names include: "OOD human interaction," "scenario" (painting), "interface (formats)," "user roles," "tasks," "analysis," and "mental model."

IE\O said this is a design issue.

MTD said this is not a modeling concept but a specialization of the problem domain concept.

Method	Comments
Booch	No
CCM	No
C/Y/N	Yes, alternative name: OOD human interaction
Demeter	Yes
Graham/SOMA	Yes
IE\O	No
MTD	Yes

Method	Comments
OBA	Yes
Objectory	Yes, alternative name: "actor"
OMT	Possibly, alternative names: "scenario" (painting), "interface" (formats)
OOIE	Yes
SE/OT	Yes, alternative names: "user roles," "tasks," "analysis," and "mental model"
SSADM4	Yes, alternative names: "user role/function matrix"
Wirfs-Brock	No
Z++	No response

Marketing concept

5 methods answered yes, 9 methods answered no.

Alternative names include critical success factor.

IE\O said this is a strategic modeling issue.

Method	Comments
Booch	No
CCM	No
C/Y/N	Yes, alternative name: "critical success factors"
Demeter	Yes
Graham/SOMA	Yes
IE\O	No, this is a strategic modeling issue
MTD	Yes
OBA	Yes
Objectory	No
OMT	No
OOIE	No
SE/OT	No
SSADM4	No
Wirfs-Brock	No
Z++	No response

Problem statement

12 methods answered yes, 1 method answered no.

Alternative names include "requirements specification," "requirements," "problem/requirements list," and "requirements catalogue."

Method	Comments
Booch	Yes
CCM	No
C/Y/N	Yes
Demeter	Yes
Graham/SOMA	Yes
IE\O	Partially, scope and requirements of analysis are defined in information strategy planning (ISP) or requirements planning (RP) stages. Scope and requirements of the system are defined in ISP or RP, but refined in analysis and user design stages
MTD	Yes
OBA	Yes
Objectory	Yes, alternative name: requirement specification
OMT	Yes
OOIE	Yes, alternative name: requirements
SE/OT	Yes, alternative name: problem/requirements list
SSADM4	Yes, alternative name: requirements catalogue
Wirfs-Brock	Yes, alternative name: requirements specification
Z++	No response

Development priority

10 methods answered yes, 2 methods answered no.

Alternative names include: "core class," "requirements catalogue," and "rank."

IE\O said this is a strategic modeling issue. OMT said that this is a system design issue.

Method	Comments
Booch	Yes
CCM	No
C/Y/N	Yes, alternative names: "core class"
Demeter	Yes
Graham/SOMA	Yes
IE\O	No
MTD	Yes
OBA	Yes
Objectory	Yes, alternative names: "rank"
OMT	Yes, but included in system design rather than analysis
OOIE	Yes
SE/OT	Yes
SSADM4	Yes, alternative name: "requirements catalogue"
Wirfs-Brock	No
Z++	No response

Does your method use alternative definitions and/or other modeling concepts in analysis modeling?

4 methods answered yes, 8 methods answered no.

Additional concepts: action diagram, actor, and scenario.

Method	Comments
Booch	No
CCM	No
C/Y/N	No
Demeter	No
Graham/SOMA	No
IE\O	Yes, action diagram, a diagrammatic representation of the actions performed by a method or a freestanding logic unit, used to provide a rigorous definition of the behavior of an operation
MTD	No
OBA	No
Objectory	Yes, actor: represents anything that interacts with the system, usually different user types; an actor has a name

Method	Comments
OMT	Yes, scenario: a sequence of events that occur during one particular execution of the system, a "typical dialogue"; used to find events and accumulate the information needed to build state diagrams
OOIE	No
SE/OT	Yes
SSADM4	No quick answer possible
Wirfs-Brock	Yes, see description of object models
Z++	No response

Conclusions

Most of the methods include a human factors concept.

Most of the methods do not use the marketing concept.

Most of the methods include the problem statement concept.

Most of the methods include the development priority concept.

Most of the methods do not have alternative definitions and/or other modeling concepts in analysis modeling.

F6   DELIVERABLES

Question

F6.1 Does your method describe major deliverables resulting from analysis modeling?

Yes/No

F6.2 If yes, give a description of these deliverables:

Deliverable _____

Description _____

Use _____

Ref./Page _____

Findings

4 methods, Booch, C/Y/N, Graham/SOMA, Wirfs-Brock indicated that analysis modeling deliverables are the same as the object modeling deliverables.

5 methods, IE\O, MTD, OBA, Objectory, SE/OT, and SSADM4, state that there are specific deliverables which are relevant to analysis modeling.

Conclusions

Is analysis modeling more than simply object modeling?

While some methods do not indicate anything additional, many methods do. Although one might argue they were "led-on" by the structure of the questionnaire, the results do indicate there is a "core" of object modeling that is common to strategic, analysis, design, and implementation modeling.

Method	Deliverables
Booch	A complete set of class diagrams which models the domain
CCM	No (1)
C/Y/N	Multilayer, multicomponent class-and-object model (2)
Demeter	Class dictionary, propagation patterns with some code fragments
Graham/SOMA	Analysis report and diagrams (3)
IE\O	Conceptual model, behavioral definitions, system definitions (4)
MTD	Requirements document (5)
OBA	Goals and objectives, analysis plan, core system activity areas, scripts, party glossary, alias table, services glossary, attribute glossary, analysis design and external issues, modeling cards, reorganization table, contract diagrams, hierarchy diagrams, state definition glossary, control flow diagrams, object dynamic model, system dynamic model
Objectory	Use case description, use case model survey, domain object model survey, domain object description, catalogue of domain objects, views
OMT	Problem statement + object model + dynamic model + functional model
OOIE	Requirements definition, object relationship diagram, event diagram, state transition diagram, prioritization analysis, design area definition, plan design
SE/OT	Problem/requirement list, static view, dynamic view, task analysis (6)
SSADM4	Logical data model, entity event model, function definitions
Wirfs-Brock	*See deliverables of object modeling* (7)
Z++	Object model diagram, structure chart, process model (8)

Notes about the table

(1) CCM: no, but does define clearly the format that one could use for the deliverables for class analysis and design.

(2) C/Y/N: exactly the same deliverables as described in the object modeling area.

(3) Graham/SOMA: see D4.1 for a list of diagram concepts:

Class Icon
Instance Icon
Classification Structure
Composition Structure
Layer
Use Structure
Association Diagram

(4) IE\O:
  - Conceptual Model = Entity (object model), and optionally an Event (control) Model and Functional Model
  - Behavior Definitions = Service Specifications and Method Descriptions
  - System Definition = The processes and object types to be supported by a system; the characteristics of that system; the development plan for design and construction. Analysis modeling may result in several system definitions.

(5) MTD: is a template structure which organizes all the problem domain and group and view concepts.

(6) SE/OT deliverables:
  - Problem/requirement list consists of list of critical requirements for the application, including nonfunctional attributes.
  - Static view consists of a diagram showing object types and their relationships.
  - Dynamic view consists of a diagram showing object behavior.
  - Task analysis consists of hierarchical task breakdown together with task characteristics (goal, frequency, constraints, etc.) and test scenarios for each task.

(7) Wirfs-Brock deliverables for object modeling are: Hierarchy graphs, Collaboration graphs, Venn diagrams (*Class cards, Subsystem cards?*) and Specification of classes, subsystems, and contracts.

(8) Z ++ deliverables:
  - Object Model Diagram is an enhanced OMT object model diagram of application domain entities.
  - Structure Chart (or ELH) is a dynamic model of the behavior of each class on the object model, expressed either in Harel notation or JSD ELH notation. All classes must use the same notation form.
  - Process Model is an SSADM4 data flow diagram of the processes for each object class on the object model.

All these deliverables are input to formal specification and design.

F7   ACTIVITIES

Question

The table on page 108 lists some activities for analysis modeling which are identified in section 7.5 of the technical framework. You should read the section before answering this question.

F7.1 Please use the table to indicate whether you use the activity in analysis modeling (answer Yes/No column).

If you have renamed this activity in your method, please give your name in the alternative name column and provide your definition of this activity.

Activity	Do you use it?	Alternative name or term
Define the problem	Yes/No	
Gather facts/Capture requirements	Yes/No	
Define the market and target environments	Yes/No	
Build a functional model	Yes/No	
Build a behavioral model	Yes/No	
Define the operations	Yes/No	
Integrate the models	Yes/No	
Review the models	Yes/No	
Redefine the problem	Yes/No	

F7.2 Does your method use other activities?
Yes/No

F7.3 If yes, give a definition of these using the following template:
Activity _____
Definition _____
How it is used _____
Ref./Page _____

Findings

All 14 respondents provided answers to this question. The table below gives a count of the number of methods that include each of the activities listed in the technical framework.

CCM does not define activities of the development process, although many of the listed activities would result in the creation or modification of CCM diagrams.

Activity	No. of methods
Define the problem	14
Gather facts/Capture requirements	13
Define the market and target environments	7
Build a functional model	6 (1 of these optional)
Build a behavioral model	13 (1 of these optional)
Define the operations	12
Integrate the models	10 (1 of these partly)
Review the models	14
Redefine the problem	11

12 methods indicated that analysis modeling included other activities.

Conclusions

There is clearly a wide range of different activities, some of which are common but most of which are different.

The depth to which each method takes the task is not addressed by the survey, and should be addressed in any future survey.

Method	Define problem	Gather facts/capture requirements	Define marketing and target environments	Build functional model	Build behavioral model
Booch	Yes	Yes	No	No	Yes
CCM	No	No	No	No	No
C/Y/N	Yes	Yes	Yes	No	Yes (4)
Demeter	Yes	Yes	Yes	No	Yes
Graham/SOMA	Yes	Yes	No	No	Optional
IE\O (10)	Yes	Yes	No	Optional	Yes
MTD	Yes	Yes	Yes	Yes	No
OBA	Yes	Yes	Yes (12)	No (13)	Yes
Objectory (14)	Yes	Yes	No for market Yes for target	No	Yes
OMT	Yes	No	No	Yes	Yes
OOIE	Yes	Yes	Yes	Yes	Yes
SE/OT	Yes	Yes	Yes	No	Yes
SSADM4	Yes	Yes	No	Yes	Yes
Wirfs-Brock (24)	Yes	Yes	Yes	No	Yes
Z++	Yes	Yes	No	Yes	Yes

Method	Define operations	Integrate models	Review models	Redefine problem	Other activities
Booch	Yes	Yes	Yes	Yes	No
CCM	No	No	No	No	No
C/Y/N	Yes (5)	No	Yes	Yes (6)	Yes (2)
Demeter	Yes	Yes	Yes	Yes	Yes (7)
Graham/SOMA	Yes	No	Yes	No	Yes (8)
IE\O (10)	Yes	No	Yes	Yes	Yes (9)
MTD	No	Yes	Yes	Yes	Yes (11)

Method	Define operations	Integrate models	Review models	Redefine problem	Other activities
OBA	Yes	Yes	Yes	Yes	No
Objectory	No	No	Yes	No	Yes (15)
OMT (18)	Yes	partly	Yes	Yes	Yes (19)
OOIE (16)	Yes	Yes	Yes	Yes	Yes (17)
SE/OT (20)	Yes	Yes	Yes	Yes	Yes (21)
SSADM4 (22)	Yes	Yes	Yes	Yes	(23)
Wirfs-Brock (24)	Yes	Yes	Yes	Yes	Yes (25)
Z++	Yes	Yes	Yes	No	Yes (26)

Notes about the tables

(2) C/Y/N: the other activities are exactly those described for the object modeling area:
   - Find classes and objects
   - Identify structure (generalization-specialization)
   - Identify structure (whole-part)
   - Identify Subjects
   - Define Attributes
   - Define Services
   - See question D6 for more details

(4) C/Y/N: this activity is named: Identify services and object interactions.

(5) C/Y/N: this activity is named: Define the services and object interactions.

(6) C/Y/N: this activity is named: Prioritize.

(7) Demeter: learn Class Structure from objects.

(8) Graham/SOMA: build an object model.

(9) IE\O: Initiate the Project: must plan which techniques and subactivities are appropriate to the project

(10) IE\O comments:
   - Define the problem—should be supplied by previous stage
   - Gather facts/Capture requirements—but not listed as a separate activity
   - Build a behavioral model = Build Event Model + Define Methods
   - Define the operations = Specify Services
   - Integrate the models—not needed since method expected to be supported by an I-CASE product
   - Review the models = Review Models and Consistency
   - Redefine the Problem = Define the System, Review Models may also redefine the scope.

(11) MTD: uses a large number of functional models to illustrate different aspects of the problem domain.

(12) OBA comment: target environment is part of objective setting.

(13) OBA comment: we capture analytic algorithms but do not build functional model as described in technical framework.

(14) Objectory alternative names:

- Define the problem = requirements analysis
- Gather facts = find actors/use cases/domain object
- Build a behavioral model = use case modeling

(15) Objectory: the names of the other activities were not supplied

(16) OOIE: alternative names:
- Gather Facts = Gather Information
- Review the Models = Confirm and Refine the Models

(17) OOIE: other activity: build a structural model, i.e., construct, based on information gathered, a model of the object types, and their interrelationships.

(18) OMT: alternative activity names are:
- Define the problem = write/obtain initial description of problem
- Build a functional model = construct functional model
- Build a behavioral model = develop dynamic model
- Define the operations = add key operations?
- Integrate the models = add key operations found in functional model
- Review the models = verify consistency, compare the three models, develop more detailed scenarios
- Redefine the problem = iterate, restate requirements

(19) OMT: other activities
- Identify Constraints between objects
- Specify Optimization Criteria
- Data Flow Diagramming included in Functional Modeling

(20) SE/OT: alternative names for activities:
- Gather Facts = critical requirements analysis
- Define the market and target environments = critical requirements analysis
- Build a behavioral model = shared object model—dynamic view

(21) SE/OT: other activities: Build an Object Structure Model (= shared object model—static view).

(22) SSADM4: alternative activity names:
- Define the problem = feasibility study
- Gather facts/Capture requirements = requirements definition
- Build a functional model = data flow modeling, function definition
- Build a behavioral model = entity event modeling
- Define the operations = entity event modeling, function definition
- Integrate the models = function definition

(23) SSADM4: no quick answer possible for other activities

(24) Wirfs-Brock: alternative activity names:
- Define the problem, Gather facts, Define the market all included in Requirements Specification
- Build behavioral model covered by Define Collaboration Graphs
- Define the Operations covered by Class Specification

(25) Wirfs-Brock: additional activities:
- Walkthrough: test various scenarios to determine what behavior needs to be distributed among the classes and subsystems

(26) Z++: additional activities:
- Build Object Structure Model: builds the object model and correlates it with the dynamic and process models

F8   TECHNIQUES

Question

F8.1   Which of the techniques identified in section 14.6 of the technical framework do you employ during analysis modeling?

F8.2   Does your method use any other techniques to perform analysis modeling activities?

Yes/No

F8.3   If yes, give a description of these using the following template:

Technique _____

Description _____

How it is used _____

Ref./Page _____

Findings

There is a wide disparity in the numbers of techniques identified, from none to almost all those listed in the technical framework—in excess of 30.

Conclusions

Many techniques are used. There seems to be some confusion as to what is meant by a technique. It is difficult to draw any useful conclusions from the responses to this question.

The technical framework needs to separate techniques, activities, and notations.

Method	Comments
Booch	All those listed in section 14.6 of the technical framework except for functional modeling
CCM	Not applicable
C/Y/N	See section D.7
Demeter	No techniques identified
Graham/SOMA	30 techniques listed for the various activities in 14.6
IE\O	23 techniques listed in 14.6 plus cluster analysis and cost-benefit analysis
MTD	No techniques identified
OBA	About 24 techniques listed from those in 14.6, plus language normalization, contract based relationships, signature definitions

Method	Comments
Objectory	Most of the techniques listed in 14.6 can be used. Their use is not prescribed by the method
OMT	5 techniques listed from those in 14.6, plus scenario preparation, testing access paths, eliminating redundant attributes and operations, iterating the analysis; shopping list operations, extracting operations from processes, events, the object model, and state actions and activities
OOIE	No techniques identified
SE/OT	15 techniques listed from those in 14.6 plus confirm subtype
SSADM4	Those listed in 14.6 except for integrate the models and redefine the problem
Wirfs-Brock	No techniques identified in 14.6. Additional techniques—heuristics for developing valid hierarchies and collaboration graphics
Z++	13 techniques listed from those in 14.6

F9 CHANGES TO THE TECHNICAL FRAMEWORK FOR ANALYSIS MODELING

Question

F9.1 Does your method identify any other feature which you think should be included in the analysis model?

F9.2 Are there features in analysis modeling which you think should be removed from the technical framework?

Yes/No

If yes, specify the feature and give your reason for its removal:

Feature _____

Reason for removal _____

Findings

Method	Comments
Booch	No
CCM	Analysis model should be split into dual life cycle: class analysis and application analysis (the dual life cycle)
C/Y/N	Additions: multilayer concept, multicomponent concept
Demeter	Addition: propagation patterns

Method	Comments
Graham/SOMA	No
IE\O	No response
MTD	Additions: MTD analysis concepts
OBA	Additions: the analysis model does not do a sufficient job calling out the need for explicit goals and objectives
Objectory	Additions: behavioral concepts; Deletions—activities, deliverables, techniques
OMT	No
OOIE	No
SE/OT	Addition: task analysis
SSADM4	No quick answer possible
Wirfs-Brock	Indeterminate/none apparent
Z++	No

Conclusions

Apart from CCM, no respondent suggested a radical change to the analysis features included in the technical framework.

8

Design Modeling

INTRODUCTION

Design modeling produces rigorous specifications of the interface provided by a set of object types.

We asked the respondents about the following:

- How is design modeling delineated in your method?
- What object structure concepts are used ?
- Which rule concepts are used?
- Which group and view concepts do you use in design modeling ?
- Which design modeling concepts are used?
- What are the deliverables of design modeling ?
- Which activities do you use for design modeling?
- What techniques are used in design modeling?
- Are there any other features that should be included in design modeling, or any features that should be dropped?

All 16 methods responded to this part of the survey.

G1   PURPOSE

Question

G1.1   Does your method specifically delineate design modeling from the other areas of the technical framework?

Yes/No

G1.2 If it does, explain how this is achieved: _____

Findings

11 methods differentiated design modeling from other areas, 5 methods did not.

Of the 11 who responded yes, 3 made a distinction between analysis along the lines of analysis being (what) and design being (how). Others defined design as a collection of different tasks such as user interface design and systems design.

Method	Comments
Booch	No
CCM	No
C/Y/N	Yes—OOD delineates via human interaction classes, task and data management classes
Demeter	No
Graham/SOMA	No
IE\O	Yes, design model is free from implementation considerations and incorporates system design considerations not found in analysis
MTD	Yes, application user interface and desktop design
OBA	Yes, design is about solutions, analysis is about capturing the problem
Objectory	Yes, design modeling is robustness analysis and design
OGROUP	Yes, what versus how
OMT	Yes, design modeling equates to system design stage
OOIE	Yes, design is how a system is built
SE/OT	Yes, application system design is user-centered, system design generates a user object model which represents the user's understanding of the objects in the system
SSADM4	Yes, but the technical framework confuses conceptual modeling with external design
Wirfs-Brock	No
Z++	Yes, corresponds to systems analysis and system design stages of Z++

Conclusions

Most of the methods differentiated analysis modeling from the other subject areas.
Many did this by taking the design modeling definition and stating how that mapped onto their method. They then stated how design in their method was different from other parts of their method.

The question forced respondents to view their methods in terms of the prescribed technical framework and this is not appropriate in all cases.

G2   OBJECT STRUCTURE CONCEPTS

Question

The table below lists some object structure concepts identified in section 15.3.2 of the technical framework. You should read the section before answering this question.

G2.1   Please use the table to indicate whether you use the concept in design modeling (answer Yes/No column).

If you have renamed this concept in your method, please give your name in the alternative name column and provide your definition of this concept.

Concept	Do you use it?	Alternative name or term
Design model object type	Yes/No	
User interface object type	Yes/No	
Business logic object type	Yes/No	
Information management object type	Yes/No	
Legacy system object type	Yes/No	
Usage relationship type	Yes/No	
Between design object type relationship	Yes/No	
Between design module relationship	Yes/No	

G2.2   Does your method use alternative definitions and/or other object structure concepts in design modeling?

Yes/No

G2.3   If yes, give a definition of these using the following template:

Concept _____

Definition _____

How it is used _____

Ref./Page _____

Findings

The answers to this question have been summarized in the following three sections.

Usage of design model object types and their specializations

	Yes	*No*
Design model object type	12	4
User interface object type	13	2
Business logic object type	9	6
Information management object type	10	5
Legacy system object type	10	5

Method	Design model object type	User interface object type	Business logic object type	Information management object type	Legacy system object type
Booch	Yes	Yes	No	No	No
CCM	Yes, class	Yes, class	Yes, class	Yes, class	Yes, class
C/Y/N	Yes/Class				
Demeter	Yes	Yes	Yes	No	Yes
Graham/ SOMA	Yes, computer system object	Yes	No	Yes, file management object	Yes, object wrapper
IE\O	No	Yes, user interface, procedure step	No, same as object model	Yes, various	Yes, subject area
MTD	No	Yes	Yes	Yes	Yes
OBA	Yes	Yes	Yes, problem domain	Yes	Yes, wrapper
Objectory	Yes, various	Yes	Yes, control	Yes, entity object	No
OGROUP	Yes	Yes	No	No	No
OMT	Not clear	No	No	Yes, data store, file, database	Yes
OOIE	Yes, implicit	Yes, presentation	Yes, policies	Yes, implementation object type	Yes, business, presentation, implementation object types
SE/OT	Yes			Yes/shared object	Yes
SSADM4	Yes	Yes, dialogue element or LGDE	Yes, entity	Yes, physical data model record	No
Wirfs-Brock	??	No	No	No	No
Z++	Yes	Yes	Yes	Yes	Yes

Relationships and their specializations

11 methods support usage relationship types, 4 do not.

8 methods support between design object type relationships, 7 do not.

7 methods support between design module relationships, 8 do not.

Method	Usage relationship type	Between design object type relationships	Between design module relationships
Booch	Yes	No	Yes
CCM	Yes, request event	Yes, request event	Yes, request event
C/Y/N			
Demeter	Yes	No	No
Graham/SOMA	No	No	No
IE\O	No	No	No
MTD	Yes	No	No
OBA	Yes	Yes, object contract	Yes, subsystem contract
Objectory	No	No	No
OGROUP	No	No	No
OMT	No	Yes, relationship between subsystems	No
OOIE	Yes, contract	No	No
SE/OT	Yes	Yes, collaboration	Yes, usage
SSADM4	Yes	Yes, vector	Yes, vector
Wirfs-Brock	Yes	Yes, collaboration, contract	Yes
Z++	Yes	Yes	No

Other object structure concepts used in design modeling

Method	Comments
Booch	No
CCM	No
C/Y/N	Yes
Demeter	No
Graham/SOMA	No
IE\O	Yes, procedure, procedure step, system, subsystem

Method	Comments
MTD	Yes, presentation object type, desktop object type
OBA	No
Objectory	Yes, entity, interface, control, design object
OGROUP	No
OMT	Yes, subsystems
OOIE	No
SE/OT	Yes, shared object model
SSADM4	No
Wirfs-Brock	Yes, walkthrough
Z++	No

Conclusions

Most methods include additional design model object types: user interface, data management, legacy system, and business logic object types were included in over half the responses.

Over half the methods mentioned additional object structure concepts within design modeling although none of them are common enough to consider adding to the technical framework.

Approximately half the methods include "between design object relationships" or "between design module relationships." These relationships, which are special to design modeling, are just part of object modeling in some methods.

The inclusion of questions about "design modeling object type" and "usage relationship object type" was confusing. These concepts were simply generalizations of more specific concepts which were included in the technical framework to complete the type hierarchy.

G3   RULE CONCEPTS

Question

G3.1   Does your method describe any new rule concepts for design modeling?
Yes/No

G3.2   If yes, give a definition of these using the following template:
Concept _____
Definition _____
How it is used _____
Ref./Page _____

Findings

Only 2 of the methods suggested additional rules: 1 used assertions to define or formalize rules, and the other defined a rule for transforming valid prior states into fail statements.

Method	Comments
Booch	No
CCM	No
C/Y/N	No
Demeter	No
Graham/SOMA	Yes, assertions (formalize rules)
IE\O	No
MTD	No
OBA	No
Objectory	No
OGROUP	No
OMT	No
OOIE	No
SE/OT	No
SSADM4	Yes, transformation of valid prior states into fail statements
Wirfs-Brock	No
Z++	No

Conclusions

From the responses it appears that design modeling does not usually involve additional types of rule. Only 2 methods describe such additions.

Most methods use rules for design and constraint management, but the additional design rules are not distinguished from object modeling rules.

G4   DESIGN MODEL GROUP AND VIEW CONCEPTS

Question

The table on page 122 lists some concepts identified in section 15.3.5 of the technical framework. You should read the section before answering this question.

G4.1   Please use the table to indicate whether you use the concept in design modeling (answer Yes/No column).

If you have renamed this concept in your method, please give your name in the alternative name column and provide your definition of this concept.

Concept	Do you use it?	Alternative name or term
Design model engineering	Yes/No	
Thread of control	Yes/No	
Concurrency	Yes/No	
Persistence	Yes/No	
Design model module	Yes/No	
Design component	Yes/No	
Design module	Yes/No	
Design quality metric	Yes/No	

G4.2   Does your method use alternative definitions and/or other group and view concepts in design modeling?

Yes/No

G4.3   If yes, give a definition of these using the following template:

Concept _____

Definition _____

How it is used _____

Ref./Page _____

Findings

These findings are summarized in the following four tables.

	Yes	No
Design model engineering concept	7	8
Thread of control	9	6
Concurrency	10	5
Persistence	12	3
Design model module	10	5
Design component	11	4
Design module	11	4
Design quality metric	9	6

5 methods included the concept of "subsystem" as a design module.

Method	Design model engineering concept	Thread of control	Concurrency	Persistence
Booch	No	Yes	Yes	Yes
CCM	No	Yes, event stream	Yes	Yes
C/Y/N				
Demeter	Yes	Yes	Yes	Yes
Graham/SOMA	No	No	Yes	Yes
IE\O	No	Yes	Yes	Yes
MTD	No	No	Yes	Yes
OBA	Yes, enforcement of objectives	Yes	No	Yes
Objectory	No	Yes, process	No	Yes
OGROUP	Yes	Yes, application flow	No	No
OMT	No	Yes	Yes	No
OOIE	Yes	No	Yes, sequential, concurrent	Yes, local, global
SE/OT	Yes	No	No	Yes
SSADM4	Yes	Yes	Yes	Yes
Wirfs-Brock	No	No	No	No
Z++	Yes	No	Yes	Yes

Method	Design model module	Design model component	Design module	Design quality metric
Booch	Yes	Yes	Yes	No
CCM	No	No	No	No
C/Y/N	No	No	No	No
Demeter	Yes	Yes	Yes	Yes
Graham/ SOMA	Yes, implementation layer	Yes, implementation layer	Yes, implementation layer	Yes, implementation layer
IE\O	No	Yes, procedure, procedure step, subsystem	Yes, procedure, subsystem, system	Yes, acceptance criteria
MTD	Yes	Yes	No	Yes

Method	Design model module	Design model component	Design module	Design quality metric
OBA	Yes	Yes, subsystem	Yes, subsystem contract view	Yes, quality objective
Objectory	Yes, package	Yes, service, simple package	Yes, package, subsystem	No
OGROUP	No	No	No	No
OMT	No	Yes, module	Yes, subsystem	Yes
OOIE	Yes, module	Yes, component, module	Yes	Yes, quality metric
SE/OT	Yes	Yes	Yes	No
SSADM4	Yes	Yes, update inquiry process model	Yes, process in a specific function model	No
Wirfs-Brock	No	Yes, component	Yes, subsystem	No
Z++	Yes	Yes	No	Yes

Use of alternative definitions and additional concepts

Method	Comments
Booch	No
CCM	No
C/Y/N	Yes
Demeter	No
Graham/SOMA	No
IE\O	Yes, dialogue flow diagram, system data flow diagram and procedure data flow diagrams, layout
MTD	Yes, dialogue model
OBA	No
Objectory	Yes, several
OGROUP	No
OMT	Yes, data flow diagrams of system
OOIE	Yes, dialogue flow, layout, event control, prototype
SE/OT	No
SSADM4	No
Wirfs-Brock	No
Z++	No

Conclusions

Persistence was the most widely supported "engineering" concept; 12 methods supported it.

Concurrency and module/component were also included in 10 or 11 methods.

Threads of control and quality metrics were included in the majority (9) of the methods.

The distinction between design model component and design module is not clear cut within the technical framework. Added to this, the questionnaire asked about support for "design model module"—it should have been "architecture concept"—and at a glance the table shows that we may as well disregard this column. But it is fair to say most methods include some sort of design module or component which is often a subsystem, but which may be a component, package, process, procedure, or implementation layer, depending on the method.

All the concepts except "design model engineering" are supported by a majority of methods, but design model engineering itself is an abstract concept created by the Special Interest Group to help manage the concept hierarchy and it may have caused some confusion.

Some methods emphasized the more general types, while others emphasized the specializations.

G5   DESIGN MODELING CONCEPTS

Question

G5.1   Does your method describe any new modeling concepts for design modeling?
Yes/No

G5.2   If yes, give a definition of these using the following template:
Concept _____
Definition _____
How it is used _____
Ref./Page _____

Findings

5 methods identify new design modeling concepts as outlined in the table on page 126. 11 methods use the existing concepts.

Method	Comments
Booch	No
CCM	No
C/Y/N	No
Demeter	No
Graham/SOMA	No
IE\O	No
MTD	No
OBA	No
Objectory	No
OGROUP	No
OMT	Yes, connection between process, processor, task, global resource, control, architectural framework, trade-off priority
OOIE	Yes, dialogue event flow
SE/OT	Yes, user object model
SSADM4	Yes, various
Wirfs-Brock	Yes, various
Z++	No

Conclusions

Surprisingly few additional concepts were offered, so most methods have been able to map their concepts into the technical framework.

These findings do not necessarily prove that the technical framework is adequate. It may simply arise because respondents tried to fit within the framework they were presented with or because their methods and issues had already been covered within the object modeling subject area.

G6 DELIVERABLES

Question

G6.1 Does your method describe major deliverables resulting from design modeling? (Refer to section 15.4 of the technical framework.)

Yes/No

G6.2   If yes, give a description of these deliverables:

Deliverable _____

Description _____

Use _____

Ref./Page _____

Findings

12 methods identify specific deliverables, 4 do not. Of the 4, 3 of them explained that refined analysis models were part of the deliverables.

Method	Comments
Booch	No
CCM	No
C/Y/N	Yes
Demeter	Yes, refined class dictionaries, propagation patterns
Graham/SOMA	Yes, analysis diagrams extended with implementation objects and library classes
IE\O	Yes, design specification
MTD	Yes, user interface style, desktop design
OBA	Yes, modified analysis deliverables, subsystem description, subsystem contract view, design prototypes
Objectory	Yes, various
OGROUP	No
OMT	Yes, structure of basic architecture for system high-level strategic decisions
OOIE	Yes
SE/OT	Yes, design schema
SSADM4	Yes, function definitions, logical dialogue designs, specific function models
Wirfs-Brock	No
Z++	Yes, formal functional specification

Conclusions

Most methods described their design modeling deliverables; 4 did not.

Some of the deliverables are refinements on preexisting deliverables. Other methods yield new definitions and/or class/object types.

G7   ACTIVITIES

Question

The table below lists some activities identified in section 15.5 of the technical framework. You should read the section before answering this question.

G7.1   Please use the table to indicate whether you use the activity in your method (answer Yes/No column).

If you have renamed this activity in your method, please give your name in the alternative name column and provide your definition of this activity.

Activity	*Do you use it?*	*Alternative name or term*
Identify design model object types	Yes/No	
Specify design model object types	Yes/No	
Identify the relations and aggregates	Yes/No	
Identify the attributes of objects and rules	Yes/No	
Specify the semantics of classes	Yes/No	
Model the behavior of the objects	Yes/No	
Combine objects	Yes/No	
Layout of the user interface	Yes/No	
Connection or mapping between the object classes and external data	Yes/No	

G7.2   Does your method use other activities?
Yes/No

G7.3   If yes, give a definition of these using the following template:
Activity _____
Definition _____
How it is used _____
Ref./Page _____

Findings

The findings from this question are summarized in the following four tables.

	Yes	No
Identify design model object types	14	2
Specify design model object types	14	2
Identify relationships and aggregates	12	4
Identify attributes of object and rules	12	4
Specify semantics of classes	13	3
Model the behavior of objects	14	2
Combine objects	11	5
Lay out the user interface	12	4
Connection or mapping between the object classes and the external data	9	6
Additional activities	6	10

Conclusions

The overall conclusion is that the technical framework provides a fair summary of the activities which are currently used in design modeling. 6 methods identified additional activities and 22 additional activities were mentioned.

We should investigate these further with a view to extending the activities list in the technical framework in any future survey of this area.

Method	Identify design model object types	Specify design model object types	Identify relationships and aggregates	Identify attributes of object and rules	Specify semantics of classes
Booch	Yes	Yes	Yes	Yes	Yes
CCM	No	No	No	No	No
C/Y/N	Yes	Yes	Yes	Yes	Yes
Demeter	Yes	Yes	Yes	Yes	Yes
Graham/ SOMA	Yes	Yes	Yes	Yes	Yes
IE\O	Yes	Yes	No	No	Yes
MTD	Yes	Yes	Yes	Yes	Yes
OBA	Yes	Yes	Yes	Yes	Yes
Objectory	Yes, find	Yes, define	Yes, homogenize or distribute behavior	Yes, define	Yes, define
OGROUP	Yes	Yes	Yes	Yes	No
OMT	Yes	Yes	No	No	No

Method	Identify design model object types	Specify design model object types	Identify relationships and aggregates	Identify attributes of object and rules	Specify semantics of classes
OOIE	Yes	Yes	Yes	Yes	Yes
SE/OT	Yes	Yes	Yes	Yes	Yes
SSADM4	Yes	Yes	Yes	Yes	Yes
Wirfs-Brock	No	No	No	No	Yes
Z++	Yes	Yes	Yes	Yes	Yes

Method	Model the behavior of objects	Combine objects	Lay out the user interface	Connection or mapping between the object classes and the external data
Booch	Yes	Yes	No	No
CCM	No	No	No	No
C/Y/N	Yes	Yes	Yes	Yes
Demeter	Yes	Yes	Yes	Yes
Graham/SOMA	Yes	Yes	Yes	Yes
IE\O	Yes	No	Yes	Yes
MTD	Yes	Yes	Yes	Yes
OBA	Yes	Yes	Yes	Yes
Objectory	Yes	Yes, package	Yes, describe	No
OGROUP	Yes	No	Yes	No
OMT	No	No	No	No
OOIE	Yes	Yes	Yes	Yes
SE/OT	Yes	Yes	Yes	Yes
SSADM4	Yes	Yes	Yes	Yes
Wirfs-Brock	Yes	No	No	No
Z++	Yes	Yes	Yes	No

Additional activities

Method	Comments
Booch	No
CCM	No
C/Y/N	Yes
Demeter	No
Graham/SOMA	No
IE\O	No
MTD	No
OBA	Architectural issue decision making, conceptual solution decision making, solution subsystem definition, solution realization decision making
Objectory	No
OGROUP	No
OMT	Subsystem, concurrency, tasks, processors, data store, global resource, control, boundary conditions, trade-off priority
OOIE	Insure referential integrity, design database structures, specify methods for computed types and relationships Specify dynamic and multiple classification, define event scheduling
SE/OT	Definition of user object model
SSADM4	Function definition, specification prototyping, logical dialogue design, physical process specification
Wirfs-Brock	No
Z++	No

G8   TECHNIQUES

Question

G8.1 Does your method describe any new techniques for design modeling? (Refer to section 15.6 of the technical framework.)

Yes/No

G8.2 If yes, give a description of these using the following template:

Technique _____

Description _____

How it is used _____

Ref./Page _____

Findings

As shown in the next table, 5 methods, IE\O, MTD, Objectory, OOIE, and OMT, all name additional techniques which are relevant to design modeling.

Conclusion

This area of methods is still developing. Methods developers should review each other's methods to see which techniques are useful and should be more widely used.

It is questionable whether the techniques listed in the technical framework can be reasonably offered as techniques. Many of the list techniques are simple "subactivities," they explain what needs to be done rather than how to do it.

Method	Comments
Booch	No
CCM	No
C/Y/N	No
Demeter	No
Graham/SOMA	No
IE\O	Yes, procedure identification; interface painting tools; dialogue flow diagrams, prototyping user interface, knowledge based procedure synthesis, joint application development workshops
MTD	Yes: user interface and desktop design techniques
OBA	No
Objectory	Yes, corresponding to the additional activities
OGROUP	No
OMT	Yes, layering, trading priorities, prototypical architectural frameworks, estimating how requirements, guidelines for files vs. database
OOIE	Yes, corresponding to the additional activities
SE/OT	No
SSADM4	Yes, but not relevant to OMG
Wirfs-Brock	No (All covered in object and analysis modeling)
Z++	Not covered by response

G9   CHANGES TO THE TECHNICAL FRAMEWORK FOR DESIGN MODELING

Question

G9.1   Does your method identify any other feature which you think should be included in the design model?

G9.2   Are there features in analysis modeling which you think should be removed from the design model?

      Yes/No

G9.3   If yes, specify the feature and give your reason for its removal.

Findings

Only 4 respondents want additional features in design modeling as shown in the table below.

Method	Comments
Booch	No
CCM	No
C/Y/N	Yes, corresponding to additions in object modeling
Demeter	No
Graham/SOMA	No
IE\O	No
MTD	No
OBA	No
Objectory	Yes, distinguish the modeling activities which consider implementation technology versus those which do not. Deletion of specific biased design modeling details and strengthen the definitions.
OGROUP	No
OMT	No
OOIE	Yes, business policies and rules
SE/OT	No
SSADM4	No quick answer possible
Wirfs-Brock	Indeterminate, none apparent
Z++	Not covered by response

Conclusions

Little useful extra material was obtained from this question, which suggests that design modeling was adequately covered by the technical framework.

One respondent asked that design modeling focus on developing an implementation independent model of a system. This was the main intent of creating this subject area of object analysis and design.

9

Implementation Modeling

INTRODUCTION

Implementation modeling takes specified (possibly system-independent) object types and develops an implementable solution taking into account: modularity, distribution, constraints, and quality requirements.

We asked the respondents about the following:

- How is implementation modeling delineated in your method?
- Which group and view concepts do you use in implementation modeling?
- What are the deliverables of implementation modeling?
- Which activities do you use for implementation modeling?
- What techniques are used in implementation modeling?
- Are there any other features that should be included in implementation modeling, or any features that should be dropped?

3 of the methods, CCM, Graham/SOMA, and OGROUP, did not respond to this part of the survey. This chapter contains the findings and conclusions from the remaining 13 methods.

H1   PURPOSE OF IMPLEMENTATION MODELING

Question

H1.1   Does your method specifically delineate implementation modeling from the other areas of the technical framework?

Yes/No

H1.2   If it does, explain how this is achieved.

Findings

3 of the 13 methods did not differentiate implementation modeling from design modeling; these were Demeter, MTD, and Wirfs-Brock.

The remaining 9 methods differentiated implementation modeling from design modeling and, as shown in the table below, explained how and why this separation occurred.

Conclusions

There is some agreement to separate implementation from design modeling.

The overall sense of the comments is that implementation is concerned with the internal design and ways in which object types are grouped together into executable modules (e.g., their modularity).

There are differences of opinion about the extent to which implementation modeling is independent of the platforms on which the objects are to run and the tools used in their development.

Method	Comments
Booch	Yes, the separation is achieved through the use of separate diagrams for subsystems and modules.
C/Y/N	Yes, in the sense that language-specific implementation strategies are included. But a second design model is not needed (or desired).
Demeter	No
IE\O	Yes, the design model concentrates on the external appearance and function of the system, while the implementation model describes the internal design of the system. Both the design and implementation models aim to be platform independent. (1)
MTD	No, combines with design modeling
OBA	Yes: OBA refers to this as detailed design. It refers to design modeling as architectural design. The distinction between the two is in the number of dependencies which exist for the decisions made in each process. (2)
Objectory	Yes, implementation design is conducted when the interface to a design object has been defined.
OMT	Yes, this subject area is equated with OMT's object design stage. Object design concentrates on getting full definitions of classes, associations and algorithms that are optimized for implementation , but without descending into particular details of an individual language or database.
OOIE	Yes, implementation addresses the construction of an executable application through building and assembly of components. Implementation includes testing of the application.

Method	Comments
SE/OT	Yes, implementation modeling is concerned with the physical implementation of objects in specific target environments, and ensuring the performance and other physical qualities are acceptable.
SSADM4	Yes, implementation modeling maps well to the SSADM4 internal design stage.
Wirfs-Brock	No
Z++	Yes, implementation modeling corresponds to the system design and systems implementation stages of the Z++ method.

Notes about the table

(1) Code generators should be able to generate systems for different platforms based on the same implementation model. Nevertheless, the target platform and user work-station capabilities will influence the choices made during design and implementation modeling. IE\O describes design in two stages: external design and internal design. Implementation modeling has been equated to the internal design stage of IE\O. The external design stage was equated to design modeling. To improve the match, the select systems architecture activity within external design has been treated as an implementation modeling activity.

(2) In architectural design, each decision has widespread effect on the system (i.e., a large number of future decisions are likely to depend on each architectural design decision. Detailed design, on the other hand, tends to focus on decisions that are far more localized, and therefore not likely to have many dependent decisions.

H2   IMPLEMENTATION MODEL GROUP AND VIEW CONCEPTS

Question

The table below lists some concepts identified in section 16.3.2 of the technical framework. You should read the section before answering this question.

H2.1 Please use the table to indicate whether you use the concept in your method (answer Yes/No column).

If you have renamed this concept in your method, please give your name in the alternative name column and provide your definition of this concept.

Concept	Do you use it?	Alternative name or term
Linkage	Yes/No	
Distribution policy	Yes/No	
Control policy	Yes/No	
Binding policy	Yes/No	
Class	Yes/No	
Quality metrics	Yes/No	

H2.2   Does your method use alternative definitions and/or other group and view concepts in implementation modeling?

Yes/No

H2.3   If yes, give a definition of these using the following template:

Concept _____

Definition _____

How it is used _____

Ref./Page _____

Findings

The following two tables summarize these findings.

	Yes	No	No reply
Linkage	9	4	
Distribution policy	10	3	
Control policy	10	3	
Binding policy	6	5	1
Class	10	3	
Quality metrics	6	7	

Method	Linkage	Distribution policy	Control policy	Binding policy	Class	Quality metrics	Other
Booch	No	Yes	No	Yes	Yes	No	No
C/Y/N	Yes	Yes	Yes	Yes	Yes	Yes	No
Demeter	Yes	Yes	Yes	Yes	Yes	Yes	No
IE\O (1)	Yes-but	No-but	No-but	No-but	Yes	No-but	Yes-but
MTD	Yes	Yes	Yes	Yes	No	Yes	No
OBA	Yes	Yes	Yes	No	Yes	Yes	No
Objectory	Yes	Yes	Yes	No reply	Yes	No	Yes
OMT	No	Yes	Yes	Yes	Yes	No	No reply
OOIE	Yes	Yes	Yes	No	Yes	Yes	No
SE/OT	Yes	Yes	Yes	Yes	Yes	Yes	No reply
SSADM4 (3)	No	No	Yes	No	No	No	Yes
Wirfs-Brock	No	No	No	No	No	No	No reply
Z++	Yes	Yes	Yes	No	Yes	No	No

Notes about the table

(1) IE\O provides the following:
  - Linkage: a strong linkage exists between persistent object types and the classes or tables in a database design. Other linkages exist between object types, their operations and the modules containing the operations. Modules are linked to systems which are linked to one or more processing environments. A processing environment defines the operating system, database system, transaction processing system, programming language, etc., used in that environment.
  - Distribution policy: not considered a "concept," but addressed in the initiate external design work and select systems architecture activities.
  - Control policy: not considered a "concept," but may be addressed in the initiate external design work activity.
  - Binding policy: not considered a "concept," but may be addressed in the initiate external design work activity.
  - Quality metrics: not considered a "concept," but quantitative criteria may be included in the design requirements and acceptance criteria agreed in the initiate external design work activity.
  - Alternative group and view concepts include: class hierarchy, data structure hierarchy, data storage hierarchy, technical architecture diagram, operation request diagram, structure chart, action block usage, and procedure action diagram.

(2) Objectory: supports public, private design object.

(3) SSADM4: implementation modeling seems to cover two SSADM stages: internal design and advice from hardware/software vendors.

Conclusions

There was broad agreement that linkage, distribution, and control were important concepts. However, there was less concurrence on the concepts of binding and quality metrics.

H3   DELIVERABLES

Question

H3.1 Does your method describe major deliverables resulting from implementation modeling? (Refer to section 16.4 of the technical framework.)

Yes/No

H3.2 If yes, give a description of these deliverables.

Findings

10 methods replied to the question. The deliverables they identified are listed in the table on page 140.

Conclusions

The deliverables described illustrate the large number of outputs from implementation modeling. Most application developers will recognize these deliverables as being similar to the outputs from their existing development processes. Most methods identify a subset of the deliverables.

The question asks whether the method describes major deliverables but did not ask respondents to say whether they agreed with the deliverables listed in the technical framework.

Method	Deliverables
Booch	No
C/Y/N	Yes, the multilayer, multicomponent class and object model, with supporting text. This includes the graphics model, the requirements and design text and ultimately the code itself
Demeter	Yes, executable programs
IE\O	Yes, implementation modules, applications; documentation is not a deliverable of this subject area; also includes logical and physical database design, designs for each object type and packaging of object types
MTD	No reply
OBA	Yes, —service descriptions/algorithms, which define the algorithms for implementing the services of an object, and are used to code that service —attribute decision cards, which describe how a logical property will be physically realized
Objectory	Yes, design object descriptions, which are used for coding and maintaining the design object
OMT	Yes, detailed object model, detailed dynamic model, and detailed functional model
OOIE	Yes, code (methods), implementation component, database definitions, test data, testing scenarios, testing results, system documentation and transition plans
SE/OT	Yes, the way in which objects are packaged into implementation components, the database design, systems documentation and user manuals
SSADM4	SSADM4 is intended for use in a large system, using a conventional database management system, and its deliverables are geared toward this. They include physical database design, update and inquiry process models, and specification models.
Wirfs-Brock	No reply
Z++	Yes, concrete application specifications which define how each abstract specification component is implemented by a class which can be mapped directly into code.

H4 ACTIVITIES

Question

H4.1 Does your method describe any activities for implementation modeling? (Refer to section 16.5 of the technical framework.)

Yes/No

H4.2 If yes, give a description of these using the following template:

Activity _____

Description _____

How it is used _____

Ref./Page _____

Findings

3 methods, Booch, Demeter, and Wirfs-Brock, did not describe any activities for this area. 9 methods did; the results are summarized in the table below and the notes which follow it.

Conclusions

Most methods provide support for the activities listed in the technical framework; however there are many suggestions for other activities to be included in the technical framework. The technical framework should be revised to accommodate the activities listed by the respondents.

Method	Activities
Booch	No
C/Y/N	Yes, see answer to D6
Demeter	No
IE\O	Yes, but there are other ways of doing it (1)
MTD	Yes, selecting user interface components
OBA	Yes, many of the activities are covered in detailed design
Objectory	Yes, see description of Objectory in Ref1 process ch 6 and Ref2 ch 7–8
OMT	Yes, but there are other ways of doing it (2)
OOIE	Yes, detailed design, construction, assemble, code, test, plan for transition
SE/OT	Yes, identify implementation modules, finalize user interface design, database design and tuning, internal; design of object operations, systems documentation

Method	Activities
SSADM4	Yes, SSADM4 is intended for use in a large system, using conventional database management system, its implementation activities are geared towards this (e.g., production of physical data model, program/data interface, update/query process models, and specific functional models).
Wirfs-Brock	No
Z++	Yes, refinement (3)

Notes about the table

(1) IE\O offers the following comments:
   - Identify policies for distribution, control and binding. Yes, addressed by initiate external design stage and select systems architecture (external design stage activities).
   - Identify implementation modules. Yes, identify load modules subactivity.
   - Define the methods. Yes, design software structure, but also done during analysis.
   - Design the details of the user interface. Yes, this is done in external design stage.
   - Design the physical details of the information management components. Yes, design data structure task.
   - Produce system documentation. No, this is a construction activity.

(2) OMT offers the following:
   - Identify policies for distribution, control and binding. Yes, probably addressed in previous stage when systems architecture is defined.
   - Identify implementation modules. Yes, package classes and associations into modules.
   - Define the methods. Yes, design algorithms to implement operations.
   - Design the details of the user interface. Yes, done at systems design stage.
   - Design the physical details of the information. Yes, done at systems design stage.
   - Produce system documentation. No, documentation decisions are included in OMT but not system documentation.

(3) Z++: for an abstract class, the definitions of more concrete state and the definition of corresponding operations and a linking predicate to form a new class which can be proved to be a refinement of the first class, using the Z++ or Z definition of data refinement.

H5   TECHNIQUES

Question

H5.1   Does your method describe any techniques for implementation modeling? (Refer to section 16.6 of the technical framework.)

Yes/No

H5.2 If yes, give a description of these using the following template:

Technique _____

Description _____

How it is used _____

Ref./Page _____

Findings

The following table summaries these findings.

9 methods commented on the techniques for implementation modeling. Some methods reminded us of the wealth of existing experience gained through the use of nonobject oriented methods. Two methods identified techniques required to create reusable classes and to actually reuse them. These techniques include: propagation, interface hiding, and refinement.

Conclusions

Many of the techniques which are used for nonobject oriented methods are still relevant in this area. More work is required on techniques to create and reuse classes.

Method	Techniques
Booch	No
C/Y/N	No
Demeter	Yes, propagation
IE\O	Yes, object to database mapping rules, access path analysis, performance assessment techniques, data storage (physical database) design option selection, packaging, technical object libraries, external modules, structured walkthroughs, encapsulating current systems techniques, action diagramming, operation request diagrams, structure charts, applying structured design principles
MTD	Yes, low-level user interface design techniques
OBA	Yes, activities covered in low-level design
Objectory	Yes, see text of Ref1 process ch 6.6; Ref2 ch 7–8
OMT	Yes, hiding external object at the system boundary by defining abstract interface classes which mediate between the system and the new external objects
OOIE	Yes, but none were specified
SE/OT	Yes, but none were specified
SSADM4	Yes, SSADM4 is intended for use in a large system, using conventional database management system, its implementation activities are geared towards this (e.g., production of physical data model, program/data interface, update/query process models, and specific functional models).

Method	Techniques
Wirfs-Brock	No
Z++	Yes, refinement for an abstract class, the definition of a more concrete state and the definition of corresponding operations and a linking predicate to form a new class which can be proved to be a refinement of a first call using the Z++ and Z rules for data refinement

H6   CHANGES TO THE TECHNICAL FRAMEWORK FOR IMPLEMENTATION MODELING

Question

H6.1   Does your method identify any other feature which you think should be included in the implementation model?

H6.2   Are there features in analysis modeling which you think should be removed from the implementation model?

Yes/No

H6.3   If yes, specify the feature and give your reason for its removal:

Feature _____

Reason for removal _____

Findings

8 respondents gave a definite "no" to this question. 3 respondents recommended that other concepts were required but only 1 explained what they were.

Conclusions

The definitions in the technical framework need improving and there are one or two things which need to be added.

Method	Other implementation model concepts
Booch	No
C/Y/N	No
Demeter	No
IE\O	No reply
MTD	No
OBA	No

Method	Other implementation model concepts
Objectory	Yes: several concepts are not readily defined, either they need more precise definitions or they need to be removed
OMT	No
OOIE	No
SE/OT	No
SSADM4	No quick answer possible
Wirfs-Brock	None apparent
Z++	Yes: verification techniques and the ability to trace requirements to implementation model components

Technical
Framework

10

Technical Framework for Object Analysis and Design

10.1 PURPOSE OF THE TECHNICAL FRAMEWORK

The technical framework is a tool for comparing object analysis and design methods. It segments object analysis and design into a number of subject areas which can be studied separately.

The technical framework seeks to find commonality between the different object analysis and design methods. It does this by using abstractions which emphasize features which are commonly found in many methods.

When applied to a specific method, the technical framework enables us to assess the extent to which that method supports the common features. However, the technical framework has to be flexible enough to enable the special features that differentiate one method from another to be described.

A technical framework is not a method.

10.2 THE FRAMEWORK

The diagram on page 150 illustrates the technical framework for object analysis and design. The shaded areas represent the subject areas covered by this issue of the object analysis and design technical framework.

The rest of this section briefly describes the components shown in the diagram.

10.2.1 Life Cycle Models

While it is convenient for this document to subdivide object analysis and design into the subject areas depicted above, development projects can package the development work in a variety of ways. We conclude that object analysis and design is particularly suited to the incremental, nonstaged life cycle models.

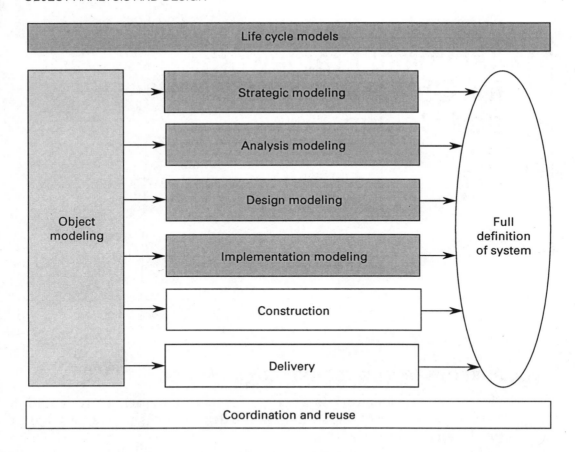

10.2.2 Object Modeling

Object modeling provides the framework, the fundamental concepts, and the techniques which unify object analysis and design. Every application developer who wants to carry out object analysis and design has to become familiar with object modeling.

Everything within the scope of object analysis and design may be thought of as an object.

Examples of objects identified during strategic and analysis modeling are: people, organizational structures, processes, real-world objects, and documents.

Examples of objects identified during design and implementation modeling are: files, windows, reports, and modules, all of which are directly related to the way in which an information system supports the users of that system.

The object modeling area of object analysis and design is based on the object model described in the Object Management Architecture (OMA) Guide.

10.2.3 Strategic Modeling

The purpose of strategic modeling is to understand the current and future intentions of an enterprise, to provide a context for future developments, and to synthesize and agree on a systems strategy while taking account of organizational, financial, and technical constraints.

Typically the results of this activity are:

- Models for the enterprise (not the systems), which cluster object types into subject areas
- A set of recommendations
- An agreed plan for systems development
- High-level systems requirements

10.2.4 Analysis Modeling

The purpose of analysis modeling is to obtain a thorough description of a problem domain, so that the requirements for applications supporting the domain can be formalized and the environment in which those applications are to be used is well understood.

Typically the results of this activity are object models of:

- Workgroups and users
- Business processes and tasks performed within processes
- Real-world objects
- Policies and rules
- Events and timings
- Constraints
- Clustering of object types into subject areas

10.2.5 Design Modeling

The purpose of design modeling is to specify the external view of an application and its associated set of object types.

Typically the results of this activity are:

- Rigorous specifications of the object types (typically object types which represent the user interface, business logic, and database components of the system and which encapsulate reused legacy systems)
- Complete specifications of operations and interfaces
- Clustering of object types into design modules
- Designs to meet quality requirements

10.2.6 Implementation Modeling

The purpose of implementation modeling is to take specified (possibly system independent) object types and develop an implementable solution taking into account:

- Modularity: which defines the approach to combining object types so that they can be ported, distributed, and managed
- Distribution: which defines the strategy for distributing object types
- Constraints imposed by hardware and software selected to deliver the implemented object types
- Quality requirements

It should be stressed that these issues are in no particular order; furthermore, this is not an exhaustive list of the issues which need to be addressed by implementation modeling.

Typically the results of this activity are:

- Complete specifications of the object types (including their internal designs)
- Clustering of object types into implementation modules

The Object Analysis and Design Special Interest Group are mainly concerned with developing implementation models which can be translated into class libraries which conform to the OMG specifications for the object model, object services, and the object request broker.

10.2.7 Construction

This is concerned with programming a set of object types to produce object classes and class libraries which will realize the implementation model.

Construction is outside the scope of this book.

10.2.8 Delivery

This is concerned with delivering the class libraries which are developed during construction to the users as part of an operational information system.

Delivery is outside the scope of Object Analysis and Design.

10.2.9 Full Definition of a System

The technical framework shows that any information system should be supported by a set of models which include:

- Strategic models
- Analysis models
- Design models
- Implementation models
- Actual classes of objects produced as a result of construction

These models provide a complete definition of the system at various levels of abstraction; furthermore, because they are all based on object models, they are readily understandable.

10.2.10 Coordination and Reuse

This subject area covers the work that is done to link the work in the different subject areas, to promote reuse of object types, and to coordinate the work of independent projects. Typical functions are:

- Asset management: which involves extracting descriptions and specifications of object types, components, and applications from systems, generalizing them and making them available to other projects

- Reuse management: which ensures that projects are aware of reusable object types, components, and applications, and that requirements to change them are actually implemented
- Development coordination: which ensures that applications are delivered in the sequence required to meet the strategic plan
- Technical coordination: which ensures that the object classes found in the operational system and object types found in an implementation model satisfy requirements identified during strategic and analysis modeling

Coordination and reuse is outside the scope of this draft of the technical framework.

11

Life Cycle Models

11.1 INTRODUCTION

A *life cycle model* describes the overall shape of the systems development process, capturing the essential management control and iteration strategies for a project.

The diagram on page 156 subdivides object-oriented development into six areas of work:

- Strategic modeling
- Analysis modeling
- Design modeling
- Implementation modeling
- Construction
- Delivery

These work areas may be viewed as *stages* of a traditional "waterfall" life cycle model.

Object-oriented methods generally eschew the waterfall life cycle model and advocate strategies such as "iterative development," "round-trip gestalt design," and "rapid prototyping."

The next section explores various strategies found within life cycle models, and proposes that object technology supports some of these strategies particularly well.

We conclude that nonstaged, incremental development has significant advantages over the waterfall approach, and is a practical choice for object-oriented development. However, object-oriented development is compatible with most life cycle models, and the life cycle model should be chosen to suit the circumstances of the project.

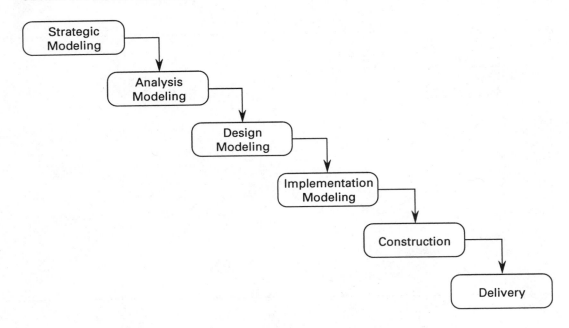

11.2 LIFE CYCLE MODEL FRAMEWORK

We shall examine the key strategies found in life cycle models, and relate them to object-oriented development.

Life cycle models can be characterized by the following:

- Iteration strategies: once-only, evolutionary, rapid prototyping, or incremental
- Packaging strategies: fixed stage, flexible stage, or nonstaged
- Progression strategies: additive or transformational
- Checkpointing strategies: rubber-stamp, management review, or risk-driven

11.2.1 Iteration Strategies

The *once-only* iteration strategy assumes that the full production system can be built the first time using one pass through all the development steps. (This is not to say the sponsor does not expect to enhance or correct or adapt the system at some future date.)

This style of development is attractive since it appears easy to manage and will cost less if all goes well. But such projects produce no assets until the entire development is complete, can suffer the "paralysis by analysis" and "sorry but you signed it off" syndromes, and are generally high risk unless the system is similar to one already developed. Team members are less motivated when delivery dates are way-off, and there are problems judging the quality of deliverables which are not working systems.

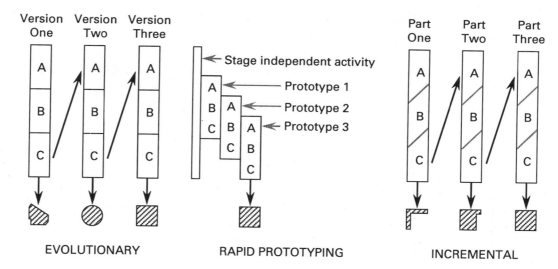

EVOLUTIONARY   RAPID PROTOTYPING   INCREMENTAL

The *evolutionary* iteration strategy assumes it will take several cycles to get a quality system, so it does not attempt to get it right the first time. Instead, rapid development techniques are employed to produce a 70%-right system, which is then exercised by the users in production or near-production mode. Successive versions of the system are built using additional cycles of the development activities, until a full-blown production system emerges.

Rapid prototyping is a variant of evolutionary development in which the cycles are faster and the scope smaller than for evolutionary development: the deliverables are used only in test mode and need not be production code. Prototyping is commonly used to evolve the user interface design, but some methods promote prototyping as a technique for discovering further elements of the problem domain.

Evolutionary development and rapid prototyping are particularly suited to system designs that involve a high degree of user computer interaction, or systems involving some new style of human interface.

The *incremental* iteration strategy involves building the system in small increments. Although it takes many passes through the development steps to build the full production system, each increment produces a useful asset. This style of development is less practical for traditional methods owing to the difficulty of merging each new increment. But application developers, by fragmenting the system into clusters of object types which encapsulate both data and operations, can develop production-quality application fragments within each cycle.

11.2.2 Packaging Strategies

The *fixed* packaging approach is one in which each *development step* is embedded in some particular stage of the method. Within such a stage there may well be alternative and optional development steps.

The *flexible* packaging approach takes the view that the development steps can be repackaged into different stages to suit the nature of the application, the culture of the company, the skills of the participants, and the available CASE tools. The diagram on page 157 assumes each cycle has been divided into three stages named A, B, and C, for example.

The *nonstaged* packaging approach does not place any management controls over the sequence of steps and their placement within stages. The two extremes of the nonstaged approach are:

- Mare's-tail waterfall, in which the stages are performed in sequence without any intervening checkpoints;
- Knowledge-based development, in which the steps are performed in any sequence, although the work is always constrained by the knowledge-base (rules of the method). For example, the rules may prevent the recording of an operation unless it can be attached to an object type; or may define what constitutes a complete and correct object definition. This style of development normally requires CASE tool support.

Nonstaged packaging is most likely to be used in conjunction with incremental development, since management controls are less necessary within short cycles. The additive nature of object models makes them more suited to nonstaged development than transformational methods.

11.2.3 Progression Strategies

A *transformational* progression means that each development stage produces a model or design, which is then transformed into a starting model or design for the next stage. Transformational progressions are problematic, since errors found, or changes needed, in earlier stages require retransformations, which typically involve destroying work done in later stages. There tends to be artificial "brick walls" between the stages and it is difficult to maintain traceability in such approaches. On the other hand, the developers are at least clear as to what stage they are working on and what their objectives are at any given time.

An *additive* progression means that each stage adds more objects and more details to the model or design produced in the previous stage. While additive development overcomes the problems of transformational progression, it is also criticized because it seemingly allows chaotic, concurrent-stage development.

The object model supports additive development as shown in the figure on page 159. Note that a transformation may still be needed to "generate" the code and database designs of the production system, as shown in the diagram. Some CASE tools, however, support *enactable specifications* (executable designs) which do not have to be transformed into code.

TRANSFORMATIONAL PROGRESSION

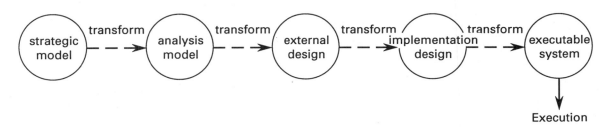

ADDITIVE PROGRESSION

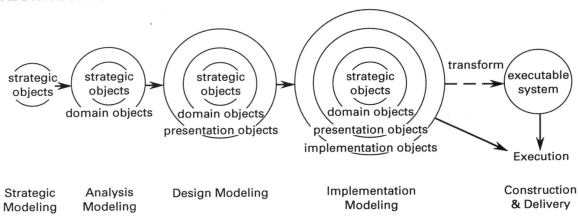

11.2.4 Checkpointing Strategies

Management checkpoints are expected at the end of each stage, and at the end of each cycle in multi-cycle development approaches.

A *rubber-stamp* checkpoint is one in which management simply give the go-ahead for the next stage or they abandon the project. Checkpoints are seldom this straightforward and a *management review* may end up re-scoping the project, demanding a reworking of a model/design or re-focusing the project in some way.

A *risk-driven* checkpoint is one in which management consciously apply formal risk reduction techniques, such as that described in Boehm's Spiral Model. As a result of the checkpoint, a different life cycle model might be adopted, or parallel projects initiated or the work recast in a radically new manner. On many occasions, of course, the decision is for the project to continue normally.

Since object oriented developments can readily use a variety of life cycle models, risk-driven checkpoints are a reasonable strategy for object oriented projects.

Object Modeling

12.1 INTRODUCTION

One of the strengths of the object paradigm is that a common core of constructs supports modeling at all levels of abstraction—from strategic modeling of real-world objects to implementation of application classes in programming languages.

This chapter describes the purpose of object modeling and the relevant concepts, types of activity, and examples of deliverables.

12.2 PURPOSE

Object modeling provides the framework, the fundamental concepts, and the techniques which unify object analysis and design. Every application developer who wants to carry out object analysis and design has to become familiar with object modeling.

The key features of object modeling which differentiate this subject area from the others are:

- Abstraction: which defines a relationship between a group of object types such that one object type represents a set of characteristics which are shared by other object types.
- Encapsulation: which implies the packaging of operations and data together into an object type such that the data is only accessible through its interface.
- Reuse: which is the ability to reuse object types during the design of a system and object classes within the implementation of a system.

- Specialization: which occurs when an object type inherits operations, attribute types and relationship types from one or more supertypes (with possible restrictions).
- Object communication: which, in object oriented systems, takes the form of one object sending requests to other objects.
- Polymorphism: which occurs when an operation can apply to several types. There are two main forms of polymorphism:
  - Inherent polymorphism: where operations are inherited by every subtype
  - Ad hoc polymorphism: where different operations on different types have the same name

12.3   CONCEPTS

12.3.1 Concept Hierarchy

The diagram on page 163 shows the concept hierarchy which contains the main concepts used in object modeling. The concepts represented in bold italics are described in this chapter.

The sections which follow identify the major groups of concepts and describe the concepts in each group.

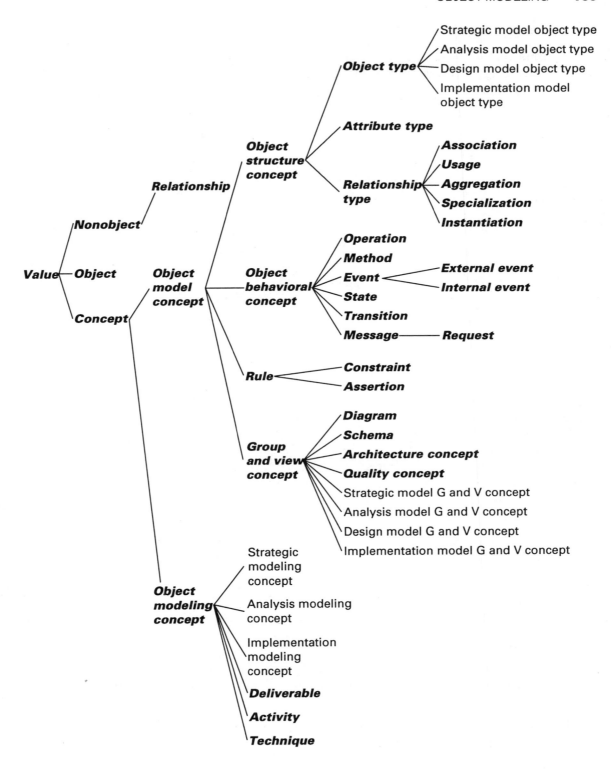

12.3.2 Values, Objects, and Concepts

This section identifies the higher level of the object model for object analysis and design. The concepts described in this section are illustrated in the diagram below:

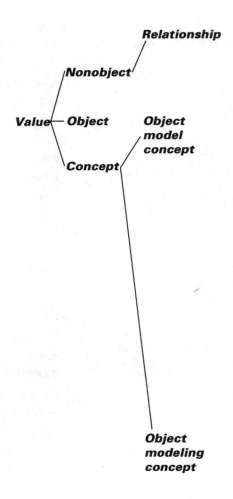

The concepts shown in this diagram are the following:

Value

Any denotable value, as described in a profile of the OMG object model which includes objects, nonobjects, and values. Typical examples of values are: '1234' and 'San Francisco'.

Nonobject

A nonobject is anything which is not an object. Each nonobject can be considered to belong to a type of value called a Nonobject type. This is analogous to objects being instances of types. Nonobjects are not labeled by an object reference and therefore cannot be the controlling argument for a request.

Examples of nonobject types defined in CORBA include: Short, Long, Ushort, Ulong, Float, etc.

Relationship

A relationship is a characteristic that specifies a mapping from one object to another; it is an instantiation of a relationship type.

Object

An object is a thing. It is created as the instance of an object type. Each object has a unique identity that is distinct from and independent of any of its characteristics. Each object offers one or more operations.

Concept

A concept is used to describe an aspect of a subject area of object analysis and design. Concepts are described in terms of a concept type hierarchy and a concept description.

The concept type hierarchy is depicted as a fern diagram where a node lower in the tree is a specialization of a node higher in the tree.

A concept is described in terms of: a brief description of the concept, characteristics (which are defining qualities of a concept), and instances (which give examples of the concept).

There are two main subtypes of concept:

- Object model concept: describes aspects of the object model.
- Object modeling concept: describes an aspect of the activities and tasks of producing object models.

12.3.3 Object Model Concepts

An object model concept underpins all object models. The set of object model concepts is represented on the diagram on page 166. It includes:

Object structure concept

An object structure concept identifies some aspect of the object types, the attribute types, and the relationship types identified during object analysis and design.

Object behavior concept

An object behavior concept describes some aspect of the dynamic behavior of the object types identified during object analysis and design. These concepts include operation, state, requests, and messages.

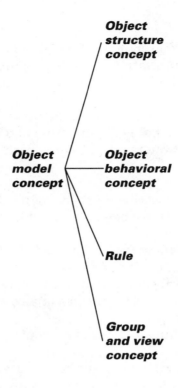

Rule

A rule can govern both the object structure and object behavior. Rules have been separated from structure and behavior because many rules address both structure and behavior. A rule can take one of two main forms—it is an assertion or a constraint.

Group and view concept

A group and view concept describes how a set of object types are grouped into a schema and/or viewed in a diagram. Concepts for grouping and viewing are treated as a single set of concepts because concepts which are used to group object types in one method are often used to view object types in another.

Specializations of grouping and view concepts include: diagrams, schemas, architecture, and techniques used to assess the quality of a system of object types (for example performance assessment charts). Strategic, analysis, design, and implementation modeling all identify specific group and view concepts.

12.3.4 Object Structure Concepts

These concepts are used to impose a structure on the object types which are identified during object analysis and design.

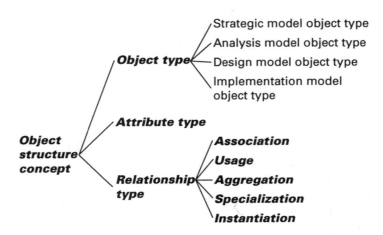

There are three concepts used to establish object structure:

Object type

An object type represents a definition of some set of object instances with similar behavior. A type is a semantic property.

Characteristics of object type are: its definition, any extension of its definition, its supertypes and its subtypes.

As shown in the diagram above specializations of object type are identified during strategic, analysis, design and implementation modeling.

Attribute type

An attribute type is a characteristic that specifies a mapping to a nonobject type. Examples of attribute type on a Customer object type would be customer name and customer address.

Relationship type

A relationship type is a characteristic that specifies a mapping from one object type to another. Characteristics of a relationship type include cardinality and optionally a range type which identifies the object types which can participate in the relationship.

An example of a relationship type is 'Borrower' defined on the type 'Copy' with a range type of 'Library User'.

There are several different types of relationship:

Association

An association is a semantic relationship with an explicit inverse relation. An example of an association relationship is 'Employer' and 'Employee' relations for the object types 'Company' and 'Person'.

Usage

A usage relationship occurs when one object type makes use of the interface provided by another object type.

Aggregation

Aggregation is a relationship such as 'consists of', 'contains', or a similar relationship between object types; it defines the composition of an object type from other object types. An example of an aggregation relationship is a 'document' contains 'text fragments' , 'diagrams', and 'spreadsheets'.

Specialization

Specialization is a relationship between two object types which represents generalization or inheritance. Object types bound by this kind of relationship share attributes and operations.

Specialization can be either single—where an object type is a specialization of one and only one object type; or multiple—where an object type inherits characteristics from more than one object type.

Specialization in a type hierarchy is commonly called subtyping/supertyping. Such relationships apply the 'is_a' nature of inheritance where the one object type 'is_a' super-type of the other. Typing is most commonly used in analysis modeling where the emphasis is on determining the *what* rather than the *how*. Typical subtyping rules define conformance between a type and its subtypes and help to resolve multiple inheritance conflicts.

Instantiation

This relationship is created when an object is created as an instance of an object type.

12.3.5 Object Behavioral Concepts

These are concepts which enable the behavior of objects to be defined.

The diagram below illustrates the set of behavioral concepts; these are described in the text on pages 168 to 169.

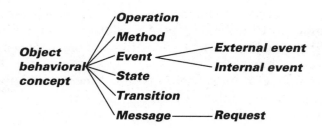

Operation

Objects support operations which may take one or more arguments, may return a result, may cause a change of state, and may trigger exceptions. An operation has a signature which contains: operation name, argument types, results types, and optionally a definition of semantics (e.g., the effect on object state).

Method

A method is that part of an object type which implements an operation. Methods are actually specified as part of implementation modeling. During strategic, analysis, and design modeling, rules and state models are used to describe semantics which will be implemented in a method.

Event

An incident which requires some response, an event denotes a specific state change within an object type. Characteristics of an event are precondition and postcondition; these denote the state of the object type before and after the event occurred, the origin of the event, and the required response. Examples of events are: 'oven overheated', 'out of stock', 'order arrives', and 'phone rings'.

External event

An external event arises from outside an object type, a domain, or a module.

Internal event

An internal event is an event generated internally within an object type, a domain, or a module.

State

The state of an object is defined by the set of values of attributes and relationships associated with that object. Associated with each state is one or more events which causes that state to change. Examples of states are: 'Waiting' and 'Ringing'.

Transition

A transition is a change of state caused by an event. An example of a transition is the change from employee to pensioner when somebody retires.

Message

A message is a communication sent or received by an object.

Messages may be categorized as either synchronous (where the message is sent from originator to receiver and the originator continues processing—as would happen between two active instances), or asynchronous (where the thread of control passes from the originating instance to the receiving instance—as would happen where both instances were part of the one overall process). Messages may also be sent in broadcast mode where there are multiple destinations. Where an overall system is distributed among several processes, which may execute on the same or separate hardware platforms, messages may be either local or remote.

Request

A request is an invocation of an operation on an object, comprising an operation name and a list of zero, one, or more actual parameters. A client issues a request to cause a service to be performed. Also associated with a request are the results that may be returned to the client.

Requests sent between object types may involve different mechanisms depending on the capabilities of the implementation language. For example, a request may employ static binding—where the destination is known at application compile-time. Conversely, a request may employ dynamic binding, where the destination cannot be resolved until application runtime. In the case of dynamically bound requests, request-sending polymorphism may result—where the same message may be sent to more than one object type. Examples of requests are: 'Get date' and 'Open file'.

12.3.6 Rule

A rule is a policy or condition that must be satisfied. An example of a rule is "for object type 'Account' account numbers must be unique."

The diagram below shows that there are two specializations of rule: constraints and assertions.

Constraint

A constraint specifies a restriction or requirement concerning instances of an object type. Examples of constraints are: the object type 'Position' has the instances 'on' and 'off'; the attribute 'part id' on the object type 'Part' must take a value.

Assertion

An assertion is a predicate that is part of the definition of an object type. An example of an assertion is "If the due date on 'Book', is later than today's date then the book is overdue."

12.3.7 Group and View Concepts

A grouping concept describes the scope of a set of object types either by itemizing the members of the set or by some representation of the membership (for example, a sheet).

A viewing concept describes different ways of representing sets of objects; usually in the form of diagrams.

Grouping and viewing concepts have been combined into a single set of concepts because the way in which object types are viewed by one method is used in another method to group object types.

The diagram on page 171 illustrates the specializations of group and view concepts; they are described the sections which follow.

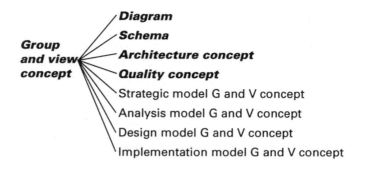

Diagram

A diagram is a pictorial representation of some aspect of a set of objects. Every diagram should have a name, a notation, a graphical representation, and semantics. There are a large number of different types of diagram used in object analysis and design.

Examples of diagrams are a type hierarchy for a bank teller machine, or an object relationship diagram for a sales order processing system.

Schema

A schema is a collection of object types and other schemas which constitute some form of operational system. Every schema identifies a list of object types; some schemas impose structure on this list.

An example of a schema is a list of bank teller object types.

Specializations of schema include: subject areas, design modules, and implementation modules.

Architecture concept

An architecture is a framework of functional components, embracing a set of standards, conventions, rules, and processes that support the integration of a wide range of information technology, enabling them to be used effectively within an enterprise.

An architecture concept is any concept which is used to create an architecture. Examples of architecture concepts include: modules, applications, and set of standards. An architecture concept is a group and view concept.

Quality concept

A quality is an assessment of the extent to which an object type, a module, or an application is meeting its requirements. Quality can be assessed from a number of different points of view including assessment of availability, usability, performance, and security.

Quality concepts are treated as group and view concepts because they help assess the effectiveness with which object types, components, and applications are integrated to form a system.

12.3.8 Modeling Concepts

These concepts are used to describe the activities and techniques used in the object modeling process. As shown in the diagram below, these concepts are specialized for each of strategic, analysis, design, and implementation modeling.

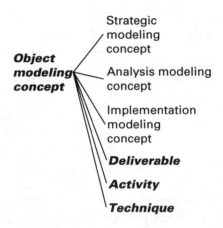

Deliverables

A deliverables is a tangible asset derived from an activity or as the end result of a process involving several activities. The technical framework only gives examples of deliverables such as a design document, a diagram or a formal textual description, or a complete executable program.

Activity

An activity gives examples of the types of activities which are typically performed in order to produce the deliverables. It should be stressed that these activity types do not constitute a design method or process.

Techniques

A technique is a set of guidelines for identifying, detailing, and verifying occurrences of the concepts and developing associations between those occurrences. Alternative techniques may exist for some activities.

Techniques may decompose into those for manipulating structural and behavioral views of a system. Techniques for developing structural views may include ways of identifying object types: abstraction; generalization and specialization; decomposition into finer and finer levels of detail; aggregation with or without lexical encapsulation; logical grouping into modules and distribution around a local or wide area network. Behavioral views of a system may involve techniques for developing message passing relationships between instances; state machines within instances; object composition from lower-level instances (logical groupings); and support for different "views" of an instance depending on particular scenarios.

12.4   DELIVERABLES

Object modeling produces generic deliverables which contain occurrences of the concepts listed above. The occurrences may be:

- Named, or given some unique identifier
- Detailed, using a number of different approaches (e.g., by using natural language, structured natural language or templates)
- Diagrammed

These will be incorporated in the actual deliverables produced during strategic, analysis, design, and implementation modeling.

12.5   ACTIVITIES

The following are the kinds of activities that may take place during object modeling:

- Discover: these activities identify sources of information.
- Identify: these activities analyze the sources of information to identify instances of the basic concepts described above.
- Organize: the concepts into the higher level concepts described above.
- Formalize: to produce the necessary deliverables.
- Review and inspect: the deliverables.
- Feedback/Refine: the deliverables to incorporate the feedback resulting from the reviews and inspections.
- Agree: the deliverables.

12.6   TECHNIQUES

The following are the kinds of techniques that may be used during object modeling:

- Interviewing
- Feedback sessions
- Facilitated group sessions
- Diagramming
- Current systems analysis
- Completeness, consistency checking
- Stability analysis

13

Strategic Modeling

13.1 INTRODUCTION

Strategic modeling seeks to provide a broad understanding of an enterprise and the domain in which it exists. It is about understanding the motivation behind, and planning to provide, a set of systems solutions within that domain.

This chapter will describe the purpose of strategic modeling, the relevant concepts, and examples of deliverables and types of activity.

13.2 PURPOSE

The purpose of strategic modeling is to understand current and future intentions of an enterprise within a domain and to synthesize and agree on a systems strategy while taking account of organizational, financial and technical constraints. Typically the results of this activity are:

- Models for the enterprise (not the systems) within a domain
- A set of recommendations
- An agreed plan for systems development
- High-level systems requirements

Examples of appropriate domains (taken from a business environment but not limited to that environment) are:

- A complete industry
- A complete enterprise
- A substantial business unit
- A specific industrial plant

- A group or set of groups with common motives
- A group sharing common concepts
- A subset of an organization's activities

The key features that differentiate strategic modeling from other subject areas are:

- Decision making: Strategic modeling is fundamentally about decision making; scoping decisions, priority decisions, investment decisions and architectural decisions. This is dependent on good working relationships between all the participants and the existence of a management forum for decision making.
- Focus on motivation: This helps clarify motivations of the people who have a stake in the enterprise and its information system.
- Integration: The broad scope of the exercise exposes the possibilities for the partitioning of coordinated projects to achieve integrated systems.
- High-level abstraction: The models developed will be a complete, but not detailed, description of the domain sufficient to understand the opportunities that exist for change, for new technology, and for reuse. The aim is to collect enough information to make intelligent decisions without incurring the expense of a detailed analysis.
- Refinement: The baseline established by strategic modeling may be selectively refined by analysis and design modeling where appropriate for systems development. The strategic model may also be iteratively refined as the domain and its environment changes.

It should be noted that strategic modeling may not be appropriate in situations where the domain is well understood or there exists a tactical need for a systems solution to a specific problem.

13.3   CONCEPTS

The basic concepts of object modeling as described in Chapter 12 (for example, object type specialization and encapsulation) are relevant to strategic modeling. Abstractions help understand the overall enterprise without considering all the details. The use of object models enables the models of the enterprise to be aligned with the object models produced in the other areas of object analysis and design. This helps understand how an information system adds value and supports the enterprise.

13.3.1 Concept Hierarchy

The diagram opposite shows the additional concepts used in strategic modeling. It represents a specialization of the concept hierarchy used for object modeling and described in section 12.3.1.

The sections which follow describe these concepts which are highlighted (by bold italics) in more detail.

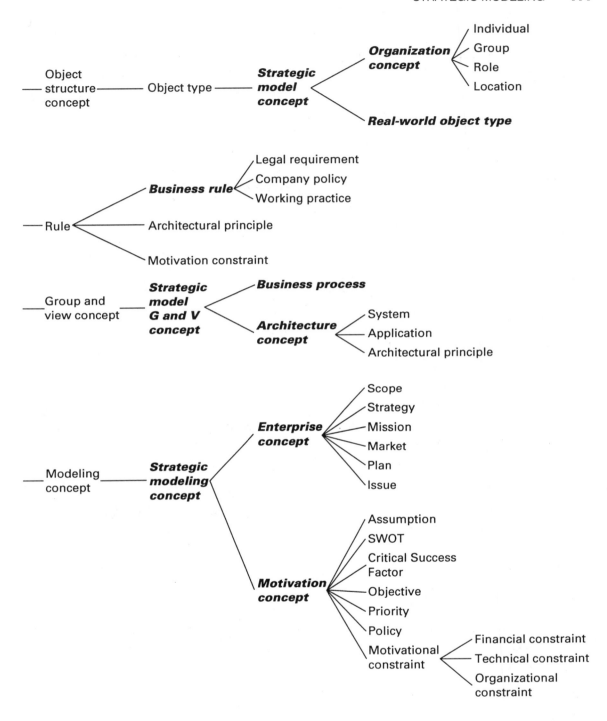

13.3.2 Object Structure Concepts

Strategic modeling introduces a number of new object structuring concepts which are illustrated in the diagram below and described in the sections which follow.

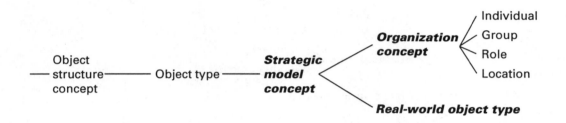

Strategic model concept

This is an additional concept used in a strategic model. Examples of these concepts are shown in the diagram above.

Organization concept

This is a concept used to describe the structure and management involved in an enterprise—an arrangement of roles, responsibilities, and individuals with a purpose. Examples of specialization of organization concept are: individual, group, role, and location.

Real-world object type

This is an abstraction of a tangible real-world object identified during strategic modeling. Examples of specializations of this object type are: Patient, Municipal Bond, and Part.

13.3.3 Rule

As shown in the diagram below, a strategic model contains specializations of rules which constrain the structure and behavior of the enterprise or organization.

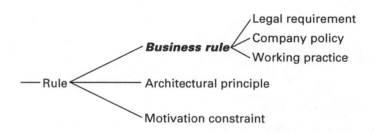

Business rule

This is a rule which governs the way that the business operates. Examples of business rules are:

- Legal requirements: for example, every enterprise must have a managing director and accountants
- Architectural principles: which govern the information system
- Motivational constraints: such as budgets and organizational limitations

13.3.4 Strategic Model Group and View Concepts

As shown in the diagram below, these concepts allow the structure and the behavior of the enterprise to be modeled by showing the relationships between the identified object types.

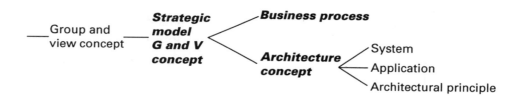

Specific group and view concepts which are found in a strategic model include:

Business process model

A business process model strives to show how the enterprise operates; it describes the relationships between the real-world object types produced and used by the enterprise, the types of departments and/or individuals who work on these object types, the types of task that they perform, and the events which trigger and control the process.

There are many different forms of business process model.

Architecture concepts

An architecture concept is used to structure the set of possible systems solutions with a view to effective planning and implementation of a solution meeting the enterprise goals.

Examples of subtypes of architecture concepts are: system, application, and architectural principle.

13.3.5 Modeling Concept

The diagram below illustrates specializations of modeling concepts used within strategic modeling.

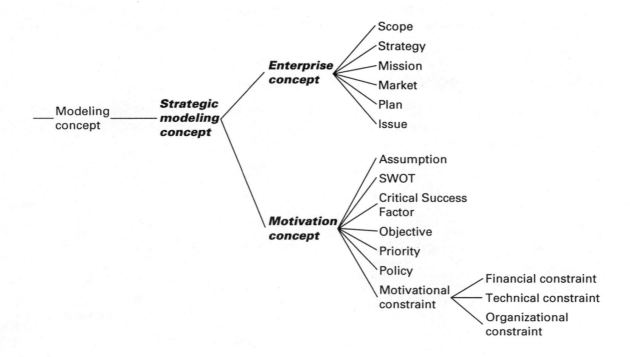

Strategic modeling concept

A concept used during strategic modeling; it is used to capture a description of some aspect of an enterprise, its behavior, and its interaction with its environment.

Enterprise concept

A concept used to describe the area of endeavor. Examples of specialization of this concept are: scope, strategy, mission, market, plan, issue.

Motivation concept

A concept used to identify a reason why the enterprise is trying to achieve a goal. Some examples are: assumption, critical success factor, objective, priority, policy, and constraint.

13.4 DELIVERABLES

This section provides examples of the deliverables that may be produced during strategic modeling.

- Statement of direction, or mission statement which embodies the objectives, priorities, constraints, and critical success factor for the enterprise
- Models which define the object types, their relationships, and behaviors
- Recommendations which may be the basis for decisions
- Issues that may be noted as risks or problems
- System boundary definitions which may be used to define the scope of the system to be developed
- Possible system architectures that would be a viable basis for systems development and integration
- Resource statement
- Development plans indicating the phasing of system development according to the resources available

13.5 ACTIVITIES

Below are listed the types of activity that may take place during strategic modeling:

- Plan
  - Define the scope for strategic modeling
  - Agree participation and responsibilities
  - Define organization and structure
- Outline
  - Identify source of motivation
  - Agree an understanding of the motivations
  - Establish a stable framework
  - Confirm strategic intent
- Understand
  - Build the object structure model
  - Build the object behavior model
  - Define processes and information (object) flows
  - Capture policies as rules
- Architect
  - Formulate candidate architectures
  - State principles
  - Examine feasibility and desirability
  - Establish management mechanisms
- Decide
  - Analyze options
  - Decide actions and define systems development plan
  - Document issues

13.6 TECHNIQUES

This section lists the types of technique that may be used during strategic modeling:

- Meetings
- Project planning
- Interviewing
- Consolidation of ideas and implications
- Strategic object modeling
- Matrix modeling
- Generic modeling
- Presentation
- Quality assurance
- Feasibility study
- Systems sizing
- Scheduling
- Resource estimation
- Data flow diagramming
- Function dependency diagramming
- Use of visual aids
- Report writing
- Tasks and deliverables
- Feedback
- SWOT (strengths, weaknesses, opportunities, and threats)
- Consensus seeking

Analysis Modeling

14.1 INTRODUCTION

Analysis modeling seeks to obtain a thorough understanding of a problem domain, by representing the real world as a collection of intercommunicating objects. This model can provides a sound basis for the design and construction of applications for that domain.

This chapter describes the purpose and concepts, and gives examples of types of activity employed in object-oriented analysis modeling.

NOTE: Since the term *system* is used ambiguously to mean a computer system or the real-world system which may have nothing to do with computers, we have used the term "problem domain" to mean a real-world system, and the term "application" to mean a computer system.

14.2 PURPOSE

The *purpose* of analysis modeling is to obtain a thorough description of a problem domain, so that:

- The requirements in the problem domain of some application can be formalized
- The environment in which those applications are to be used is well understood

The key features of analysis modeling that differentiate it from the other subject areas are:

- **Freedom from design and implementation considerations:** The analysis model is free from design and implementation considerations. This aids clear thinking, and means the one model can be used as the basis for alternative designs and implementations. In practice, the model may reflect some design and implementation decisions where these are "givens" of the problem definition.

- **Scope:** The *scope* of analysis modeling is typically the scope of a proposed new application. But it may extend wider than the application, so organizational, interfacing, and environmental implications are better understood. It may be a fragment of a proposed application, since incremental development is favored. It may be the scope of several potential applications so the shared database and application integration requirements can be better understood.
- **Creates a rich picture:** of the problem domain which embraces both the social environment in which the applications are to be used and a range of potential technical applications.
- **Reuse:** The analysis model can reuse or specialize objects obtained from libraries or earlier projects. Opportunities for generalizing the model are sought and incorporated into the model.

14.3   CONCEPTS

14.3.1 Concept Hierarchy

The type hierarchy below lists the principal concepts employed within analysis modeling. An item in bold italics indicates that the concept is described in this chapter.

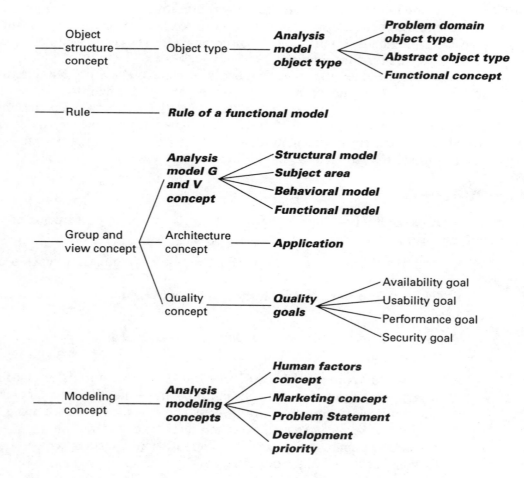

14.3.2 Object Structure Concepts

These concepts are used to structure the object types in the problem domain. They describe the "things" of the problem domain, in a design and implementation-independent manner.

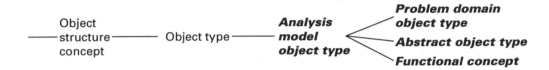

The object structure concepts used in an analysis model are illustrated in the diagram above. They are:

Problem domain object type

This is a tangible or conceptual real-world object type. Examples of problem domain object types are:

- For commercial domains: Customer, Accident, Budget
- For engineering domains: Sensor, Motor, Oven

Certain properties of the problem domain object type may be documented. For example:

- Object type name
- Definition/description
- Identifiers
- Rules (e.g., integrity constraints)
- Number of instances
- Persistent *or* transitory
- Visibility

Abstract object type

This is an abstraction used to group common characteristics of real-world object types.

Functional concept

This is a concept used to build a functional model of the problem domain. Examples of functional concepts are:

- For commercial domains: Accounting, Open_New_Account
- For engineering domains: Plant_Control, Fill_Tank

Some functional concepts may be (later) recognized as operations.

14.3.3 Rules

Analysis modeling identifies specific rules which apply to the object structure and object behavior models. In addition to these rules, analysis models also contain rules which apply to functional models.

———Rule——————— ***Rule of a functional model***

Rule of a functional model

This is a principle which constrains the behavior of a functional model. Examples of this type of rule are pre- and postconditions which constrain the order of activities within a functional model.

14.3.4 Group and View Concepts

These concepts are used to group and view analysis models.

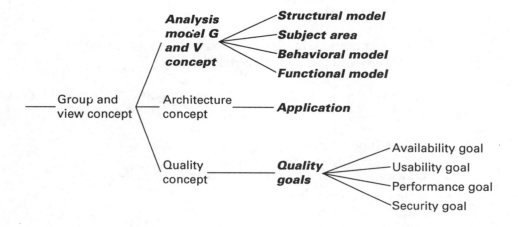

Structural model

A structural model describes the structure of the object types in the problem domain.

Examples of structural models are:

- Object relationship diagram
- Type hierarchy
- Whole-part diagram
- Subject area relationship diagrams

Typically, in these models, the nodes depict object types and the arcs depict relationships. Some diagramming conventions allow attributes and operations to be shown on the diagram. Some representations allow specialization, instantiation, and usage relationships to be shown. Various adornments are used on the arcs to depict facts about the relationships.

Separate diagrams may be used for each type of relationship (e.g., type hierarchies show specialization relationships).

Subject area

A subject area is a subset of a problem domain. They are used to clarify a complex problem domain.

Separate diagrams may be drawn for each subject area, or a subject area may be collapsed into one node, or superboxes drawn round subject areas. Further diagrams may then be used to show the interrelationships between subject areas.

Behavioral model

A behavioral model describes the dynamics of the object types within the problem domain. Examples of behavioral models are:

- Event list
- State transition diagrams
- Life cycle diagrams
- Event (communication/consequence/flow/dependency) diagrams
- Event trace, scenarios
- Use case models
- Object request diagrams

Functional model

A functional model describes problem domain processing, with more emphasis on process inputs and outputs and actions than on the events and "things" of the domain. It may also structure the activities into a functionally based framework which may be useful when communicating the model and during design.

Examples of functional models are:

- Functional decomposition diagrams
- HIPO charts
- Data flow diagrams

A functional model concentrates on problem domain activities and the fact they support higher-level activities/functions. HIPO charts also cover inputs and outputs, while data flow diagrams describe the sources and destinations of inputs and outputs, including *data stores*. Functional models originated in structured analysis methods and are less prevalent in object analysis and design methods.

Examples of functional models are: the process model for filling in an income tax return and the task model for sending a document via electronic mail.

Application

An application is a part of an information system which is used to deliver business functionality.

Quality goals

Quality goals are measures that can be used to ensure that an information system or an application meets the requirements of its users.

It is possible to define quality goals for the availability of the system, its usability, its performance, and its security.

14.3.5 Modeling Concepts

These are concepts which are used during analysis modeling; they do not form part of the analysis model.

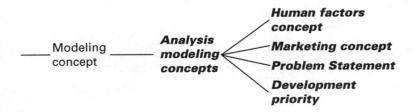

Human factors concept

Any concept used in human factors modeling, which describes the people who operate within the problem domain, and their interface and training requirements for the application(s) to be developed. Examples of human factors concepts are:

- User role hierarchy
- Learning model
- Teaching model

Marketing concept

Any concept used when building marketing models, which describe the market for the application(s) to be developed. Examples of marketing perspectives are:

- Service opportunities from selling the product
- Key benefits of the product

Problem statement

A description of the scope, purpose, planned applications, and development constraints which are relevant to the analysis modeling effort.

Considerable variation in the *problem statement* is possible. It may be non-existent at the start of analysis modeling, and is developed during analysis modeling.

Here is an example of what a problem statement may contain at the end of analysis modeling:

(a) The broad scope of the problem area;
(b) The current problems that any application must solve;

(c) Application operational characteristics: e.g., ease-of-use, reliability, availability, maintainability, performance, data integrity, and these should be quantified;

(d) Interfaces to be supported;

(e) The production/runtime platform(s) to be supported;

(f) The physical environment for the application;

(g) Design constraints, which may include financial constraints;

(h) The problem domain activities to be supported and, sometimes, the problem domain data to be supported by the planned application(s);

(i) Any assumptions made in the analysis;

(j) Any issues/loose ends.

Development priority

These concepts are used to prioritize the order of development of the object types and functional capabilities identified in the analysis object model.

14.4 DELIVERABLES

Some form of *problem statement* is a prerequisite for analysis modeling.

An *object structure model*, along with the redefined problem statement, is the minimum deliverable from analysis modeling. The most likely output from analysis modeling is some form of requirement document. The actual name given to such a document depends on the method being used and the culture of the enterprise which creates it.

Many of the group and view concepts take the form of diagrams, and these may have associated "dictionaries" or "filled-out templates" which provide additional details about the object types appearing in the diagram.

14.5 ACTIVITIES

Here are some examples of typical activities that might be used during analysis modeling:

Define the problem

Gather facts/capture requirements

Define the market and target environments

Build an object structure model

Build a functional model

Build a behavioral model

Define the operations

Integrate the models

Review the models

Redefine the problem

While these activity types have been listed in a possible sequence, we are not attempting to convey a preference for any particular sequence.

A project could make many "passes" through its activities: various extremes are:

- A single pass, since the entire problem domain is analyzed before progressing to design, although internal iterations may be needed as a result of a review activity
- A planned number of passes, because the problem domain is subdivided into subjects, subsystems, subdomains, or increments
- A large, unknown number of passes, since the development style chosen is analyze-a-bit, design-a-bit, implement-a-bit

14.6 TECHNIQUES

This section provides examples of how the above activities might be performed.

Define the problem

No examples provided in the orginal survey.

Define the market and target environments

No examples provided in the orginal survey.

Gather facts/capture requirements

Interviewing

User workshops

Current systems analysis

Reading

Domain analysis (not application specific)

Observation

Prototyping (to determine problem, not the design)

Object categories

Use case, scenario

Kelly grids

Card sorts

Build an object structure model

Generalization/looking for patterns

Language analysis (looking for nouns, verbs, etc.)

Modifying stereotyped domain models

Specializing library objects

CRC cards, templates (form-filling)

Layered object model

Role synthesis

Build a functional model

Functional decomposition

Functional hierarchies

Data flow diagramming

Dependency diagrams

HIPO charts

Operation categories

Stereotyped processes/services

Build an object behavioral model

Event analysis

Life cycles of objects

State transition analysis

Simulation of a chain of events

Role analysis

Define the operations

Object request diagramming

Mapping from problem domain activities

Functional decomposition

Operation logic definition techniques:

- Free text
- Structured, procedural language
- Action diagrams
- Declarative specification/rules
- Structure charts
- Object request charts
- Flow charts
- Stereotyped (standard) operations
- Jackson-style process models
- Programming language syntax

Integrate the models

Role synthesis

Round-trip-gestalt development

CASE tool support

Review the models

Prototyping (to check analysis results, not the design)

Completeness checking (object/operation matrices, comparison with existing systems, comparison with problem statement)

Consistency checking (checklists, rules associated with the analysis method, automated checking)

Normalization

Robustness checking/impact analysis

User workshops

Structured walkthroughs

Redefine the problem

Prioritization techniques

Design Modeling

15.1 INTRODUCTION

Design modeling produces rigorous specifications of the interfaces provided by a set of object types.

This chapter describes the purpose of design modeling, the relevant concepts, and examples of deliverables and types of activity.

15.2 PURPOSE

The purpose of design modeling is to specify the external view of a set of object types. Typically the results of this activity are:

- Rigorous specifications of the object types (typically object types which represent the user interface, business logic, database components of the application and encapsulate reused legacy applications)
- Complete specifications of operations and interfaces
- Clustering of object types into design modules
- Designs to meet quality requirements

The key features of application design which differentiate it from the rest are:

- **Specifications:** of each object type so that all its interfaces (e.g., operations) and its states are fully defined
- **Object type inheritance:** which is used to improve the consistency and performance of a set of object types and to minimize development costs

- **Components of an application:** design modeling focuses on segmenting an application into design modules which support the user interface, business logic, and information management aspects of the application.
- **Grouping of object types:** into design modules
- **Reuse:** of existing designs either in the form of existing object types or existing legacy components encapsulated as object types

15.3   CONCEPTS

15.3.1 Concept Hierarchy

The hierarchy below shows the concepts over and above those identified in Chapter 12 which are used in design modeling. The rest of this section describes the concepts which appear in bold italic in more detail.

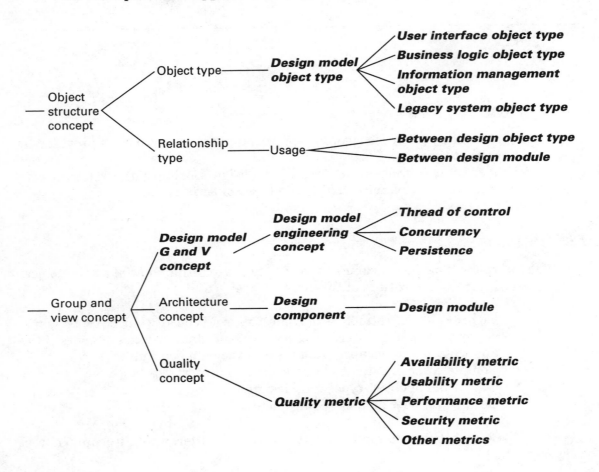

15.3.2 Object Structure Concepts

The concepts which are added to those described in Chapter 12 are illustrated in the diagram on page 195 and described in the sections which follow.

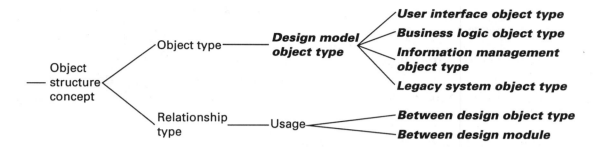

Design model object type

This is an object type which is used in a design model. Specializations of this object type are used to design the different components of the application. Examples of some of the specializations of design object type are:

User interface object type

This is an object type used to define the user interface for the application. Specializations are:

- Presentation object types which describe the visual appearance of the user interface
- Dialogue object types which maintain the state of the interface and from the user's perception controls its overall behavior
- User interface metaphors which ensure that users can understand the user interface

Examples of presentation object types are: the chart of today's stock usage, a box object, a line object, and a tree object. An example of a dialogue object type is the open file dialogue provided by a word processor.

Business logic object type

This is an object type which provides the functionality of the application. They are usually representations in the application of real-world object types.

Information management object type

This provides persistent storage for the application. Specializations of this object type are:

- Storage object types which manage the actual storage
- Integrity model object types which maintain the overall integrity of the storage object types

An example of an information management object type is a record definition in a logical database design.

Legacy system object type

This object type encapsulates an existing non-object-oriented application or application component, by defining an object-oriented interface so that it can be reused. Every system containing encapsulated legacy applications generates subtypes of this object type.

Usage relationship type

The need to specify object types leads to a need to provide clearer descriptions of the relationships between object types. Examples of these new relationship types are:

Between design object type relationship

This type of relationship describes how the object types interact at runtime. A between design object type relationship exists if one object type makes requests on another object type or if an object type creates events for another object type.

Between design module relationship

Design modeling integrates object types together into design modules. A between module relationship identifies the requests which are passed between design modules.

15.3.3 Object Behavior Concepts

Design modeling does not introduce any additional types of behavior concept.

15.3.4 Rules

Design modeling does not introduce any additional types of rule.

15.3.5 Group and View Concepts

The diagram below illustrates the group and view concepts used in a design model.

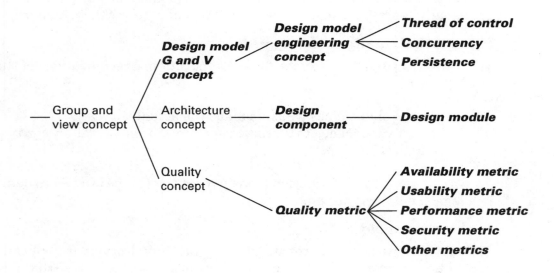

Design model engineering concept

A concept used to ensure that the application provides the functionality that users require.

Thread of control

A thread of control defines the line of independent dynamic action within an application. A given application may simultaneously support many different threads of control, which come into existence and cease to exist dynamically.

Engineering an object-oriented application requires an understanding of the different threads of control.

Concurrency

This is a property which differentiates an active object from one which is not active. Active objects encompass their own threads of control.

Persistence

This is a property of an object by which its existence transcends time (i.e., the object continues to exist after its creator ceases to exist). Characteristics of a persistent object type are: state which is made persistent, an interface which enables persistence to be controlled. Instances of persistent object types: a stored sales record and a stored pixel image.

Design model module concept

This is a concept which enables the modularity of the application to be defined. There are two specializations of this concept.

Design component

This is a collection of object types which create a single unit of functionality.

Design module

This a collection of design components which are integrated together. A design module is itself a design component.

Design quality metric

A set of measures which define the estimated quality goals which are expected from the design components and modules.

There are a number of specializations of design quality metrics. These vary because of the different ways used to measure the different qualities. These specializations include metrics for availability, usability, performance, and security and other measures.

Note: these are not actual goals; these can be generated only by testing the actual installed application.

15.3.6 Design Modeling Concepts

As yet, design modeling does not introduce any new design modeling concepts.

15.4 DELIVERABLES

Design modeling produces deliverables which are typically specifications of the object types which need to be used to create the application.

These specifications identify:

- Existing object types which are to be reused in this application
- Specialization of existing object types
- New object types
- Encapsulated legacy applications

15.5 ACTIVITIES

In general the process of design modeling mirrors activities which occur in analysis, but focuses directly on the specification of abstractions, object types which will eventually implement the model.

Important design modeling activities include:

- **Establishing the application architecture:** which scopes each application, establishes the applications architecture, and identifies potential design modules
- **Identifying the design model object types**, and generalizations and specializations of those object types and the relationships and aggregates (inverses, part-whole) which occur between them (e.g., students attend classes)
- **Designing the user interface:** as a set of graphical object types and a specification of its relationship to the problem domain objects
- **Designing persistent object types**
- **Encapsulating existing applications and data**
- **Modeling the behavior of the object types:** by constructing event diagrams and/or state transition diagrams to model the behavior of the application at a general level (i.e., not specific to a particular object type) and mapping this to the operations and requests supported by specific object types
- Specifying the object types: including their attribute types, relationship types, operations and states
- Specifying the design modules: as reusable combinations of object types
- Reviewing quality of the design: to ensure that it meets the required quality goals

At the conclusion of the design modeling the application developer should have rigorous definitions of all aspects of the application. With these in hand, specific design decisions and trade-offs regarding actual implementation of the object types, interfaces, and storage systems will be made during implementation modeling. Thereafter, depending on the power of the method during the code generation and construction phase, an executable application (to a degree) will be produced. It is worth noting that newer tools and methods stress the need for simulation and/or direct execution of the model constructed by the method (obviating the need for a construction phase, other than regular systems integration and testing).

15.6 TECHNIQUES

This section provides examples of how the above activities might be performed. They are in no particular order.

Establishing the application architecture

This is a top-down activity which involves:

- Structuring the object types into applications
- Scoping each of the applications
- Identifying the architecture which applies to all the applications
- Identifying common standards which apply to all the applications; this includes the user interface and database standards

Identifying the design model object types

- Identifying the object types within each application
- Identifying the specialization relationships to understand inheritance relationships in the operational system
- Identifying the relationships and aggregations which occur between object types
- Modularizing the object types to maximize the reuse of existing object libraries

Designing the user interface

- Identifying the metaphors which are to be used to support the user interface
- Identifying the real-world object types which need to be made visible at the user interface and their possible visual representations
- Selecting appropriate user interface runtime components and development tools
- Designing the user interface presentation object types by considering the available user interface object types (e.g., windows, etc.) and the concurrency required at the user interface
- Deriving the application dialogue model from the functional model
- Designing the object types for the user interface component

Designing persistent object types

- Identifying the object types which need to be persistent
- Selecting appropriate information management runtime components and development tools
- Designing the storage object types and the integrity rules which they are to support
- Designing the object types for the information management component

Encapsulating existing applications and data

- Selecting the existing components
- Identifying the services that they need to support
- Identifying object types which will represent them

Modeling the behavior of the object types

- Constructing event diagrams for the application
- Constructing state transition diagrams for the application
- Identifying the requests required by each object type
- Identifying the operations supported by each object type
- Developing a usage model which confirms that all of the requests and supported by operations
- Identifying the threads of control though the object types and the design modules

Specifying the object types

- Identifying the attribute types on each object type
- Identifying the relationship types associated with each object type
- Identifying the operations supported by each object type
- Developing a state model for each object type
- Defining the protocol to control the requests supported by the object type

Specifying the design modules

- Defining the scope of the design modules
- Reviewing the object inheritance model in each design module
- Minimizing the interface supported by the design module as a step toward making it reusable
- Establishing if and how the design module can be reused

Reviewing quality of the design

- Reviewing the quality goals to ensure that they are correctly stated
- Reviewing the resulting system design from the point of view of the quality goals
- Carrying out quality assessments

16

Implementation Modeling

16.1 INTRODUCTION

Implementation modeling provides a set of concepts which will facilitate the configuration of distributed and modular applications. It is about the need to ensure that the application meets its objectives in terms of qualities.

This chapter will describe the purpose of implementation modeling and the relevant concepts, examples of deliverables and types of activities.

16.2 PURPOSE

The purpose of implementation modeling is to take specified (possibly platform independent) object types and develop an implementable solution taking into account:

- **Modularity:** which defines the approach to combining object types so that they can be ported, distributed and managed
- **Distribution:** which defines the strategy for distributing object types
- **Constraints:** imposed by hardware and software selected to deliver the implemented object types (e.g., classes)
- **Quality requirements**

The key features of implementation design which differentiate it from the rest are:

- **Modularity:** which defines object types which can be bound together into implementation modules
- **Distribution:** of implementation modules within the platforms and processes of the delivery system
- **Specific quality criteria:** which must be met by the delivered system

16.3 CONCEPTS

16.3.1 Concept Hierarchy

The hierarchy below shows the main concepts used in implementation modeling. One of the features of this model is that there are no new object structure, behavior, or rule concepts. There are, however, new group and view concepts; those that are highlighted (bold and italic) are described in the section which follows.

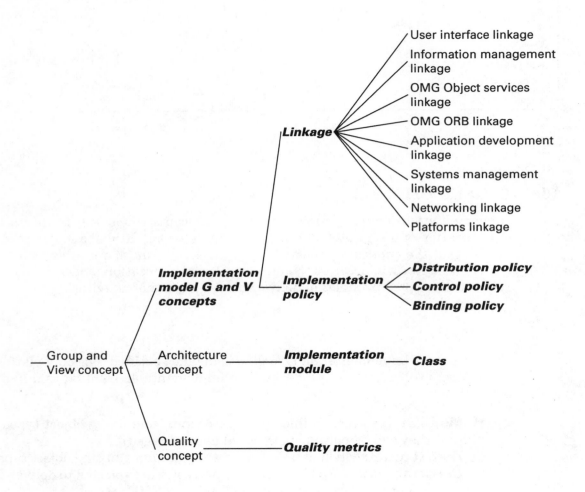

16.3.2 Group and View Concepts

Linkage

A linkage is an association between an object type in an application and the infrastructure used to deliver that application. A linkage contains information which either specializes object types supported by infrastructure so that they meet the needs of the application or specializes object types of the application so that they can adapt to the needs of the infrastructure.

Within the OMG architecture a linkage maps an application into the common facilities, object services and object request broker.

There are separate linkages between the user interface, business logic, information management and legacy system object types of the application and the supporting infrastructure which includes components for user interface, information management, object services and platforms.

The use of linkages is controlled by the tools used to develop and manage the application (e.g., application development and systems management tools).

These linkages take different forms. For example, there are many ways to structure and store persistent data: should all persistent data be stored in a database or will the capabilities of the programming language be used to store and retrieve data? These issues are addressed by physical database design which is a particular form of linkage.

Distribution policy

A distribution policy dictates the overall implementation architecture. Implementation modules are composed of object types and may be formed in many ways, depending on the distribution policy adopted.

Some possible distribution policies are:

- A single implementation module handles all instances of all object types in the system.
- An implementation module may handle all instances of just some object types in the system; other object types are handled by other implementation modules.
- More than one implementation module will handle instances of several object types.

Control policy

The flow of control through a system is important in implementation modeling. This involves both communication between object types and communication between modules of object types. Communications may be either synchronous or asynchronous depending on the object types involved.

Examples of such policies are those concerning access to persistent data. In the case of data storage in a DBMS, the data access may largely be controlled by the DBMS, although there is still potential for logically encapsulating data with access methods where the access methods interact with the DBMS.

Binding policy

A binding policy defines the extent to which the object types are bound together during construction or their bindings are left until later. The implementation of this policy has a marked impact on the ability to reuse object types and components.

Class

A class is a description of a group of objects (instances) with similar properties, and common behavior, semantics, and relationships. A class represents a particular implementation of an object type. A class is composed of two parts—namely an interface and a body. The interface defines the services which that class offers to users. The body is the detailed implementation of the class. It is internal structure not visible outside the class itself.

Quality metrics

An implementation modeling quality metric is a quality metric based on an implementation design which includes most of the signifiant design decisions which impact availability, performance, and security.

16.4 DELIVERABLES

The output from implementation design is the complete specification of:

- **Implementation modules:** which are targeted at specific types of infrastructure
- **Applications:** in terms of the implementation modules which are used to deliver them
- **Documentation:** about how to integrate, deliver, and use them as part of a working system

16.5 ACTIVITIES

In general the process of implementation design mirrors activities which occur in design modeling, but focuses on the implementation of the object types, modules, and applications.

Important implementation modeling activities include:

- **Identifying the policies for distribution, control, and binding**
- **Identifying implementation modules:** which implement the policies identified above
- **Defining the methods:** on object types
- **Designing the details of the user interface:** screen designs, etc.
- **Designing the physical details of the information management components:** including identifying indexes and other access paths
- **Producing system documentation:** including user manuals, help screens, installation instructions, and instructions for module and application reuse and integration

16.6 TECHNIQUES

This section gives examples of techniques which support the activity types which are impacted by object technology.

Identifying the policies for distribution, control, and binding

- Review the constraints identified by strategic and analysis modeling.

Identifying implementation modules

- Review the quality requirements for availability and performance.
- Duplicate functionality in implementation modules to provide enough capacity to meet the quality requirements.

- Carry out evaluations to confirm that availability and performance requirements are met.

Defining the methods on object types

- Specify methods to implement the rules, state models, and operations identified in the design model.

Designing the details of the user interface: screen designs, etc.

- Lay out presentation object types using the user interface guidelines identified as part of the information technology strategy or during design modeling.
- Carry out evaluations to confirm that the user interface meets the user requirements.

Designing the physical details of the information management components

- Review the availability and performance requirements.
- Design access paths.
- Design index structures.
- Carry out evaluations to confirm that the availability and performance requirements are met.

Producing system documentation

- Use the analysis object structure as a basis for the user documentation to describe the concepts behind the application.
- Use the functional model as a basis for the user documentation to describe what the application can do.
- Use the dialogue model as a basis for the user documentation to describe how to use the application—typically this information should form the basis for the help screens.
- Use the design and implementation models to provide the instructions for installation, integration, and module and application reuse.

Further Reading

Note: OMG documents are available from Object Management Group, Framingham Corporate Center, 492 Old Connecticut Path, Framingham, MA, 01701-4568, USA.

TO CREATE THE TECHNICAL FRAMEWORK

The following is a list of documents used in the compilation of the technical framework.

Booch 1

Method of Object Analysis and Design, from Rationale, OMG document 92.1.7

Booch 2

Object-Oriented Design with Applications, by Grady Booch, Benjamin Cummings, Redwood City, CA.

Cadre

Teamwork, by Cadre Systems, OMG document 92.1.4

Coad 1

Object Oriented Analysis (Second Edition), by Peter Coad and Ed Yourdon, Prentice-Hall, Englewood Cliffs, NJ, 1991

Coad 2

Object Oriented Design, by Peter Coad and Ed Yourdon, Prentice-Hall, Englewood Cliffs, NJ, 1991

DWays 1

Design Ways, from Design Technology Support, OMG document 92.1.6

Fowler

A comparison of OO methods, slides by Martin Fowler, 1991

Fusion

Method developed by Hewlett-Packard Laboratories, Bristol, Great Britain

Hewlett-Packard

An Evaluation of Five Object-Oriented Development Methods, by Patrick Arnold et al., SIG Publications, New York, 1991

IE\O

Information Engineering with Objects, from Texas Instruments, OMG document 92.1.13

Martin/Odell

Object-Oriented Analysis and Design, James Martin and Jim Odell, Savant Books

MTD 1

Marketing to Design: Response to OMG, from ICL, OMG document 92.1.12

MTD 2

Marketing to Design: Identifying a High Value Solution, available from ICL

OMG 1

Object Management Architecture Guide, 1989, available from OMG

OMG 2

Common Object Request Broker, 1991, available from OMG

OMG 3

Object Services Architecture, 1992, available from OMG

OORASS

Object Oriented Role Analysis, Synthesis and Structuring, Taskon A/S., OMG document 92.1.16

OOSE

Object Oriented Software Engineering, from Objective Systems, OMG document 92.1.1

Osmosys

OSMOSYS, from Winter Partners, OMG document 92.1.3

PTech

PTECH, from Associative Design Technology, OMG document 92.1.5

RDD

Responsibility Driven Design, described in *Designing Object-Oriented Software*, Rebecca Wirfs-Brock, Wilkerson and Wiener, Prentice-Hall, Englewood Cliffs, NJ, 1990

Rumbaugh

Object-Oriented Modeling and Design, Rumbaugh et al., Prentice-Hall, Englewood Cliffs, NJ, 1991

Shlear/Mellor 1

Object Lifecycles: Modeling the World in States, S. Shlear and S. J. Mellor, Prentice-Hall, Englewood Cliffs, NJ, 1992

Shlear/Mellor 2

Teamwork Support, from Cadre Technologies Inc., OMG document 92.1.4

Versant

Versant Design, from Versant Object Technology, OMG document 92.1.2

SURVEY RESPONSES

These documents contain the survey responses for the different methods. As with the rest of the survey, they are in order of method short name.

Booch

Object-Oriented Design with Applications (Booch Method), Rationall's response to the Object Analysis and Design Group's Survey of Methods, OMG document 92-12-3, available from OMG

CCM

Class-Centered Modeling, Eric Aranow, CASElode Consulting. Mr. Aranow's response to the Object Analysis and Design Group's Survey of Methods, OMG document 92-12-12

C/Y/N

Coad/Yourdon/Nicola: Survey responses . . . Prepared for the OMG's Object Analysis and Design SIG, Peter Coad and Mark May. Available from OMG

Demeter

The Demeter Method and the OMG Reference Model, Karl J. Lieberherr, Northeastern University. Description of the Demeter Method as a response to the Object Analysis and Design Group's Survey of Methods. OMG document 92-12-4

Graham/SOMA

The SOMA Approach, Ian Graham. Mr. Graham's response to the Object Analysis and Design Group's Survey of Methods. OMG document 92-12-3

IE\O

Texas Instruments' Response to the OMG Object Analysis and Design Survey of Methods, John Dodd, Texas Instruments. Texas Instruments' response to the Object Analysis and Design Group's Survey of Methods. OMG document 92-12-7

MTD

Marketing to Design, Andrew Hutt, ICL. ICL's response to the Object Analysis and Design Group's Survey of Methods. OMG document 92-12-1

OBA

Object Analysis and Design: Survey of Methods 1993: Response for Object Behavior Analysis (OBA), Kenneth H. Rubin. Available from OMG

Objectory

Objectory's Response to Survey of Methods, Magnus Christerson, Objectory. Objectory's response to the Object Analysis and Design Group's Survey of Methods. OMG document 92-12-2

OGROUP

OGROUP Method, Loredana Mancini, Olivetti Information Services. Olivetti's response to the Object Analysis and Design Group's Survey of Methods. OMG document 92-12-21

OOIE

Response for James Martin & Co. for Information Engineering. Available from OMG

Rumbaugh

OMT/Rumbaugh Method, John Dodd. Available from OMG

SE/OT

Systems Engineering for Object Technology (SE/OT), David Redmond-Pyle, LBMS. LBMS's response to the Object Analysis and Design Group's Survey of Methods. OMG document 93-1-1

SSADM4

Object Analysis and Design Survey of Methods 1992: SSADM4 Response, Graham Berrisford, Model Systems. CCTA's response to the Object Analysis and Design Group's Survey of Methods, prepared by Model Systems. OMG document 92-12-5

Wirfs-Brock

Response for Wirfs-Brock, Brad-Kain. Available from OMG

Z++

Object Analysis and Design: Z++ Survey Response, K. Lano and H. Haughton. Available from OMG

Index

DATE DUE

OCT 31 1996		
DEC 4 1996		
REC'D DEC 0 4 1996		

|